Inside Out Transformation®
presents

The Energetics of Money Liberation™

The PLAY*book*

Support For Your *Money Liberation Project*

Linda Humphreys, PhD

THE ENERGETICS OF MONEY LIBERATION™ ~ The PLAY*book*

Support for Your Money Liberation Project

www.DrLindaHumphreys.com

Published by Inside Out Transformation, LLC

The contents in this book are not meant to diagnose medical and/or psychological problems. Neither the work I do nor the information presented within this book are a substitute for medical attention and care, psychological counseling, financial counseling and consulting, legal advice, and/or psychiatric care. No guarantees or claims are made regarding diagnosing, cures, clearings, releasing, and/or healings.

The information provided in this book is strictly for the purposes of energetic and spiritual awareness. If you choose to apply the ideas provided within this book, you are taking full responsibility for your actions.

Unless otherwise noted, all Bible quotations are from the King James Version (KJV), accessed through *www.biblehub.com.*

ISBN-13: 978-0-9724161-7-7

Names: Humphreys, Linda, author.
Interior Designer: Pam Terry
Editor: Candace Johnson
Proofreader: Michelle C. Booth
Front Cover Original Illustration Artist: Paitoonpati
Book Cover Designers: Linda Humphreys and Erik Allen
Back Cover Photographer: Melody Barooni

Printed in the United States of America

This book is dedicated to

Seekers,

Believers in redemption,

more than second chances—and choosing again, Dreamers,

Strivers,

Transformers,

Visionaries,

Way-Showers,

and

Those who persist in the quest of capital "T" Truth both Within and Throughout—

in everything and everyone.

Yesterday I was clever, so I wanted to change the world.
Today I am wise, so I am changing myself.

~ Rumi ~

Are you able to receive merely "pennies" from Heaven—
or are you ready—
as a child of the Most High—
to receive your divine birthright inheritance—which can include
financial liberation and prosperity?

—Dr. Linda Humphreys

Contents

Introduction

The Energetics of Money Liberation™ ~ The PLAY*book—Support for Your Money Liberation Project,* is a thoroughly detailed and methodically laid-out program. It is a detailed expansion of what was presented in the parent book, *The Energetics of Money Liberation ~ 6 Steps for Finding and Releasing Your Blocks to Experiencing Financial Liberation NOW!*

The parent book is meant to be read first. It explains the background and rationale for this type of exploration. It also explains the reasons behind the modalities I have chosen for this program. While there may be some minor duplicate content in both books about divining and clearing procedures, the PLAY*book* provides additional procedural information and subconscious statements (both "Lack of Positive" and "Negative / Challenged")—and is presented in a workbook format. the PLAY*book* provides literal space in which you can journal, document, track, and keep information about your process and progress in a detailed and contained manner.

Some of the elements I value in an instruction book—related to any topic—and the criteria I used to discern if something is a good fit or match for me—are as follows:

- **Practicality**
    - *Is this topic important to me?*
    - *Is what is offered something that I want in my life?*
    - *Will the quality of my life be enhanced, in some way and on some level, by investing my money, time, energy, and effort into it?*
- **Simplicity and Efficiency**
    - *Though the information is perhaps unfamiliar and*

different from what I have ever heard, known, or experienced up to now, is it presented in a clear manner?

- *Are any procedures or protocols well defined and clearly laid out?*
- *Are the directions broken down in easy-to-follow steps?*

These elements (and more) are some of the guiding influences that informed the writing of the PLAY*book*.

To get the most out of the PLAY*book,* I recommend you follow each and every step in the order in which it is presented. There is a reason for following the steps that lead up to the actual discovery and clearing / releasing of the subconscious programs / energy blocks and imbalances. That reason is to create a gentle yet solid and lasting foundation—with supportive methods and steps—through which you can enhance your own relationship with money.

Prior to beginning your project, I suggest you read "Questions and Responses" in the back of this book. Becoming familiar with some things that may happen along the way (for example, the same energetic statement that was cleared keeps coming up to be cleared again) will be extremely beneficial. If nothing else, know that the Questions and Responses section is meant to be used as a tool for support and guidance while you are doing your own *Money Liberation Project*.

Speaking of doing this for yourself, I have created this program so you can actually do everything by yourself and for yourself. If you would like additional supportive coaching assistance and want to book private coaching sessions, visit www.DrLindaHumphreys.com.

May *The Energetics of Money Liberation™ ~ 6 Steps for Finding and Releasing Your Blocks to Experiencing Financial Liberation NOW!* and this PLAY*book* support you in achieving new and greater levels of financial prosperity and liberation.

PART I

PROJECT PREPARATION

Chapter 1

What Lies Within—
and How It Relates to Your *Money Liberation*

What lies behind us and what lies before us are tiny compared to what lies within us. —*Ralph Waldo Emerson*

I wanted to see what the Bible says about what lies within. Below are two very clear statements that address this. The first passage is as follows:

> And when he was demanded of the Pharisees, when the kingdom of God should come, he answered them and said, The kingdom of God cometh not with observation (20): Neither shall they say, Lo here! or, lo there! for, behold, the kingdom of God is within you. (21) (Luke 17)

Here is another verse that is extremely clear about what lies within:

> *Know ye not that ye are the temple of God,* and that the Spirit of God dwelleth in you? (16) If any man defile the temple of God, him shall God destroy; for *the temple of God is holy, which temple ye are.* (17) (1 Corinthians 3, emphasis mine)

Who We Truly Are

This psalm undeniably declares who we truly are:

> I have said, Ye *are* gods; and all of you *are* children of the most High.
> (Psalm 82:6, emphasis mine)

In the Old Testament, it is noted that when someone wanted to commune with God, they went to a physical temple. In the New Testament, we are reminded that **we** *are the Temple of God, and as such, we embody Holiness Within.*

*We are also told that the Kingdom of God is not something to be passively observed and outside of ourselves—it is within us—***all** *of us. So ... go within, consciously connect with God's Holiness—your Holiness Within—and connect with the Kingdom of God which is always present within you.*

The power of inside out transformation resides within! And so it is ...

—Dr. Linda Humphreys

You Already Are

As children of the Most High, we are inherently endowed with the power to create and experience miracles. Miracles, as defined by *A Course in Miracles*, can be a shift in perception.

You have a birthright as a child of the Most High.

- *You already are* what you are seeking (Love).
- *You already have access* to what you are seeking (Divine Guidance, miracles, loving, support, and so on).
- *You already possess* what you are seeking—so own it, tap into it, use it, express gratitude—and share with others.

First, however, you must own that

- ***YOU*** are a Beloved Child of God;
- **God *adores YOU*** and wants only the best for you; and
- Within you lies the power to transcend and transform any and all situations and circumstances—including your financial status.

Because of who your Divine, Adoring Creator and Parent is—and created you to be—you do have "entitlement." You are *entitled* to miracles. Miracles are your birthright—and as such, they are your right to create and experience—including miraculous transformations with your relationship with money.

It is your choice whether to own this as your Truth and experience—or not. If you choose not to accept and own this, your divine potential will remain dormant. Remember: nothing changes if nothing changes—especially your perceptions and resulting life experiences.

If, however, you decide to own your divine miracle-creating nature as your True Divine Nature—and consciously choose aligned perceptions, take divinely inspired and aligned actions, and live accordingly—strap on your seat belt; you are in for an amazing ride—an even better adventure and experience than what you could even imagine.

Chapter 2

How to Consciously Connect with Spirit / Inner Guidance Within

First and foremost, know this: we—*all of us*—are always connected with Spirit / God / Inner Guidance Within. ***Always.*** This does not necessarily mean that we are *consciously* aware of this fact. Some people may even protest that they do not "feel" or think that they are always connected with God. Our connection to God is not something that we turn on and off. The only thing that we do turn on and off is our conscious awareness and acceptance of this fact. Having said that, this chapter is written to provide assistance with making a *conscious* connection to God Within you.

How to Approach Queries for More Heart- and Soul-Centered Answers

While queries could easily be answered "off the top of your head" (coming from your thinking-mind), the intention here is to go within and seek a deeper connection and discover the answers that come from a deeper place—your Heart and Soul. (I am capitalizing the "H" in "Heart" to signify the Heart of God Within and not one's physical heart. I am also defining Soul as "God Within.")

Prior to doing any type of "within" process, I found it imperative to take some proactive measures to secure both maximum quality time and clear, positive results. These steps involved addressing both my outer and inner environments. Below are the preparation steps I took.

Outer Environment

- Informed those within my home environment that I would be taking a break. I informed them that I needed a quiet space and did not wish to be disturbed for a while and would reconnect with them when I was ready to do so. I asked them to please not disturb me during this time.

- Chose a quiet and comfortable room
- Posted a "Please Do Not Disturb" sign on the door before closing the door
- Had my favorite pen and journal handy
- Found a comfortable space within the room
- Sat down and relaxed
- Turned off my cell phone

NOTE: Muting the phone's ringer is not sufficient, as the phone could still vibrate and cause a disturbance of the process.

Options: None of what I have listed below is required. These options are simply things that, at times, I explored.

- Lighting a contained candle
- Playing soft instrumental music or vocalizations with no lyrics to distract my mind
- Lighting incense

NOTE: When doing this kind of exploration, I prefer silence. Other people do a more ceremonious "ritual" prior to doing this kind of work.

In this context, I am defining *ritual* as an outward pronouncement, through demonstration, of setting up both the outer and inner environments, with the intention for sacred and reverent connection. It is outside of my ordinary—signifying that what is about to happen consciously opens me up to the extraordinary. It gives notice to both the mind—*all* the minds (conscious / thinking-mind, unconscious / subconscious mind, busy / ego mind, the mind of consciousness)—and the senses that something out of the habitual routine is about to happen. It signals the minds to take notice and come in alignment with what will occur next.

ANOTHER NOTE: For the remainder of this PLAY*book*, when I instruct you to do this specific process, I will simply refer to it as ***Preparation: Outer Environment***. This is always done with Preparation: Inner Environment.

Inner Environment

Next, I prepared my inner environment by following these steps:

- Closed my eyelids
- Placed my hand in the area of my heart
- Stated my intention to go within in a peaceful and gentle manner

NOTE: What is key is to set an intention to connect within and then simply trust the process—regardless of what your thinking-mind (which can influence your body) is telling you.

- Took a slow, deep breath through my nose
- Released breath in a slow, deep manner through my mouth

NOTE: The goal is to achieve long, deep, and extended breathing—fully engaging the entire torso.

- Repeated the step above three or more times, as the goal and my intention were to achieve a more relaxed state and establish a connection within
- Tried to take notes of impressions, words, and images that arose while my eyelids were still closed
    - If I was not able to do so, I waited until I ended the process and then immediately journaled what came forward.

ANOTHER NOTE: For the remainder of this PLAY*book*, I will refer to preparing both environments (which is imperative to do prior to starting each and every step—especially the clearing and releasing steps), as ***Preparation: Outer & Inner Environments***.

Meditation = Listening to God

Simply stated, meditation means *listening* to God / Spirit / Highest Power. It does not mean listening for what you hope to hear. Meditation is not about manipulating anything to get a specifically desired outcome. It is not meant to uphold or support your thinking-mind's thoughts, stories, perceived "wrongs," and other misperceptions.

Meditation is about being open and vulnerable enough to accept whatever comes forward without interference from the thinking-mind. It is also about a willingness to listen for and to hear Truth (capital "T") rather than what the thinking-mind / ego / personality / human wants to label as truth and wants to hear. It is a time to turn within and tune into your Intuition, which I believe is the Voice of God. It is meant to liberate you from the thinking-mind and support you in connecting with the Mind of God Within.

While meditation is often described in various ways, including a "mindfulness" practice, for those new to the concept and practice, you can view it in these ways:

- Meditation is a mind-*less*-ness practice—It is an opportunity to practice disconnecting from the head chattering / monkey mind / munching mind—creating stillness within to be open to not only perceiving God's Inner Guidance but also being able to clearly attune to it.
- Mediation is a mind-*full*-ness practice—After being able to quiet the chattering mind, it creates space in which you can connect with The Oneness—and *fill* your mind with The Mind of God.

Either way, meditation is a practice—and requires practice. When I make it a habit to meditate—even for a few minutes on a regular basis—I find that my body and my psyche actually begin to crave doing it. I feel a bit "off" if I do not take a few minutes to simply attune inwardly and be still. The more I meditate, the more I want to meditate.

How to Begin to Meditate

Quiet your mind. Tune in to the rhythm of your heartbeat, or to the rise and fall of your chest, while you deeply inhale and exhale.

If your attention wanders and you begin to engage with your thinking-mind, be gentle with yourself and simply return to the stillness within.

Optional: At the beginning of the meditation, you can state your intention to receive inner knowing about a specific topic. You can also ask a question, request guidance, information, support, and/or inspiration.

Energetic Qualities of Meditation

- Openness / vulnerability
- Acceptance
- Willingness
- Humility (see Chapter 5 in *GETTING GOD® ~ "The GOD Project"—6 Steps for Divining Your Way to a More Intimate & Loving Relationship with God.*)

Examples of Meditation Queries (Optional)

- What does Spirit / God / Highest Power want to reveal to me about money?
- What does money want to communicate to me about money?
- How can I become more ________________?

More About How I Connected Within / Meditation Support

In addition to taking the steps above, I imagined my heart connecting with the Heart of God / Spirit / Highest Power. At times, I imagined our hearts being connected with a golden cord. Sometimes I imagined God's Heart expanding and enveloping me. Additionally, there were other times I imagined God's Energy being akin to the sun, however God's Energy became so huge, bright, and powerful that it melted away everything—and yet we melded together.

Regardless of what imagery came forward, I placed my hand on my own heart to literally feel it beating. This helped me to slow down my thinking-mind and slowed down my breathing, which created a more relaxed state.

SUGGESTION: If you are not familiar with or experienced in this kind of process, my advice is to just keep going. Do not depend on a specific "feeling" and then judge yourself for not reaching the exact state you were expecting. Even those who have been *going within* and connecting with the inner self for years have shared with me that sometimes they sense an immediate connection ... yet other times ... well, not so much. That statement accurately depicts my experience as well.

Here are some tips for staying aware and consciously connected to your inner environment and getting the maximum benefit from your "going within" / meditation experiences:

- Even if your mind wanders, simply try to observe these passing thoughts in a neutral manner. Do not engage or "feed" the thoughts. Simply take another deep breath in and out, and try to disconnect from the thought. Let it pass. Re-establish your connection to your heart-center within.
- Consciously state your intention to *go within*.
- Take in and release more deep breaths.

- To focus and center within, you can also silently state a simple one-word mantra repeatedly. Try some of the examples below:
  - *Flow ... Flow ... Flow ...*
  - You can also state a one-word mantra with each in breath and with each out breath.
    - An example: Say with each in breath: *Thank you.*
    - With each out breath: *I Am grateful.*
- Be open to responses in the form of ideas, impressions, sensations, colors, sounds—the various multisensory ways your Inner Knowing / God Within can reveal Itself—*plus* messages and information to you.
- Always have a pen and a journal close at hand.
- Again, if possible, try to take notes of impressions, words, and images that arise while your eyelids are still closed. If you are not able to do so, wait until you end the process and then immediately journal what came forward.

How I Ended My Going Within Sessions

- Prior to completion, I would take a final deep breath while:
  - slowly opening my eyelids, and
  - silently expressing gratitude to Spirit / Inner Knowing for our time / my conscious connection time together.
- I would then immediately journal about whatever came forward.

Chapter 3

Tracking Your Inner State

As a metaphysical scientist, I found that during my *Money Liberation Project*, documenting observations through tracking how I was feeling and what I was thinking about money—and my perceived relationship with money—was extremely beneficial.

Devising a rating scale was something I dabbled with during various times in my life. When I became a student in the master's degree program at University of Santa Monica (USM), during the Relationship Project course (in which I chose God as my focus), each student had to create his or her own individual rating scale. My 1 to 9 rating scale, with 1 as the lowest / worst / most negative perception and 9 as the highest / best / most positive perception I could conceive of was a revelatory process. I decided to connect within to my inner child and allow that younger aspect of myself to assist with the rating scale creation process. (By the way, 10 allowed for something even better than I could possibly imagine. I did not want to define, contain, or limit it, so I just left that open as a constant possibility.)

I had fun creating my rating scale. Here were my low-, mid-, and high-range rating criteria for my "My Relationship with God" exploration:

How I Feel about God and My Relationship with God Today

1. I am doomed and will be sent to hell.

5. Things are looking up. Instead of going to hell, I will probably end up going to purgatory.

9. God and I are One. God is Love. I love God. God loves me.

Similarly, I created a rating scale for my *Money Liberation Project*.

How I Feel about Money and My Relationship with Money Today

1. I am doomed and will die in debt and penniless.

5. Things are looking up. Instead of dying penniless, I will probably end up on working on a "poor farm."

9. Money gravitates to me like a magnet. I am experiencing an ever-increasing flow of financial resources and fun—and I am grateful!

Additionally, for both projects, I created various rating scales and charts to track different variables. Here are some of my *Money Liberation Project* variables:

- Overall quality of the relationship / proximity I perceive regarding my *money liberation*
(daily rating using a nine-point scale and charted as *R / P*)

- Level of yuck! (anxiety, fear, and anger / resentment) versus inner peace, calm, and confidence I'm aware of inside when I'm thinking about money
(daily rating using a nine-point scale and charted as *Y / IP*)

- Level at which I am experiencing *money liberation*
(daily rating using a nine-point scale and noted as *ML*)

- Number of times I experience perceiving *money liberation* as achievable and possible my life
(daily counting variable and noted as *A + P*)

SUGGESTION: You can create your own spreadsheets and track each variable separately, if you choose. Additionally, you can print calendar pages from a large calendar. You can easily mark each day during your *Money Liberation Project*, as I did for my variable ratings:

January

12			
R: 6	F / L: 5	G = L: 5	Pr: 7

BOTTOM LINE: Though this process is optional, I highly recommend doing some form of tracking. I was pleasantly surprised by and delighted to observe the progress I was making during my USM course's Relationship Project. At the completion[1] of the course, it was fun to compare before and after snapshots of where I was within.

Remember that the point is to have fun. Make this a simple, easy, light, and supportive process.

[1] I use the term *completion* to mean the completion of my USM course's Relationship Project. However, your *Money Liberation Project* as presented in the book ***THE ENERGETICS OF MONEY LIBERATION ~ 6 Steps for Finding and Releasing Your Blocks to Experiencing Financial Liberation NOW!*** and **the PLAY*book*** can and should continue, if and when you detect and discern that there are other energy statements to clear. In other words, it can be an ongoing and open-ended process.

Optional: *What would you like to track? What are your variables?*

1.

2.

3.

4.

Optional: *What would you like to track? What are your variables?*

1.

2.

3.

4.

Optional: *What would you like to track? What are your variables?*

5. (Mid-Level)

6.

7.

8.

Optional: *What would you like to track? What are your variables?*

9.

10. (Highest)

Chapter 4

Energetic / Spiritual Tool Kit

I believe we should all have, and can use, a myriad of different spiritual / energetic skills as tools.

Prayer

One of the essential tools in your Energetic / Spiritual Tool Kit is prayer.

Prayer is actually talking to God—and not just delineating a wish list and/or a list of grievances about people, places, and things. It is your Soul connecting with God's loving essence.

After studying different types or forms of prayer, I decided to experiment and change how I prayed. In this chapter are some of the things I learned and believe contribute to a greater sense of connectedness while praying.

Energetic Qualities of Praying

- Honesty
- Openness / vulnerability
- Willingness to transform
- Affirming
- Gratitude
- Trusting God / Spirit / Highest Power
- Flexibility

Elements to Include While Praying

- Address God.
- Express gratitude.
- Speak from your heart.

- Express humility (see Chapter 5 in *GETTING GOD® ~ "The GOD Project"—6 Steps for Divining Your Way to a More Intimate & Loving Relationship with God*), acknowledge God as God / Spirit / Highest Power, and express gratitude for God's presence and prominence in your life.
- Acknowledge openness to God's infinite wisdom and divine plan for everyone and everything involved in the situation.
- Listen.
- Express even more gratitude.
- Affirm: *Thank you. I am grateful. And so it is. Amen!* (or something akin to that).
- Trust God and allow for the best for all Souls involved to transpire.

Example of Prayer for Greater Conscious Connection

God / Spirit / Highest Power, I am grateful for this time to commune with You. I am open and receptive to bringing forth whatever can be cleared and released and will make a significant difference in my releasing, healing, and transformation—particularly as it relates to my relationship with and experience of money—at this time. I know You are with me and guiding this process in an easy and gentle manner. I pray for deeper understanding, greater awareness, and opening up to Your loving presence in my life—and the experience of *money liberation now.*

(Listen.)

Thank you for Your love and support, now and always. I affirm this and even more delightful and joyful experiences, for my greatest benefit and for the greatest benefit of all others as well. Thank you. I am grateful.

And so it is. Amen.

Now it is time for you to create your own prayer.

Steps

- Prepare: Outer & Inner Environments (see Chapter 2).
- Internally, state your intention / make your declaration or claim.
- Example of a declaration / claim: "Here is my powerful, heart- and soul-aligned prayer that invokes what I want to experience regarding my relationship with money—and my *money liberation*—and how it relates to myself and others."
- Begin writing.

My Prayer

(Write your prayer below.)

My Prayer (cont.)

Optional: Create an Ideal Visual Touchstone

Being a visual person, I like to surround myself with things that inspire and delight me. Listed below are some tools I have used during my *Money Liberation Project* that are creative, inspirational, and actually fun to create. Doing them helped set the vibrational tone for what I wanted to experience.

Vision Board

Collect pictures and words or phrases from magazines, calendars—anywhere—of the kind of emotions you would like to experience. When you look at a certain image, it should invoke the feeling of what you are seeking.

Materials Needed

- Pictures, photos, words, and phrases
- Poster board
- Glue stick
- Optional: markers, crayons, other craft materials (if you want to add dimension)

Steps

- Prepare: Outer & Inner Environments.
- Internally, state your intention / make your declaration or claim.
- Example of a declaration: "I Am creating a vision board that invokes what I want to experience regarding my relationship with money—and my *money liberation*—as it relates to myself and others."
- You can invoke your playful inner child to assist you in this activity.
- Create a collage that fills you with inspiration and delight.

  - o You can also draw with crayons, colored pencils, pens, or finger paint.

- Enjoy!

Place your work of art and inspiration in a place that is prominent (for you). Ideally you will see it the first thing in the morning and before you go to bed at night.

Mandalas ("Sacred Circle")

Mandala is a Sanskrit word meaning *circle*. Essentially anything contained within a circle can be considered a mandala. In this context, a mandala can be used to contain representations or symbols of the *money liberation* and financial prosperity that are meaningful for you.

Materials Needed

- Select a piece of paper, poster board, or canvas.
- You can choose what you prefer to use: colored pens, acrylic paint, watercolors, or crayons—or you can use a combination.
- Ask your playful inner child to pick the colors to use in coloring your mandala.
- Optional: Use something to support you in drawing a circle (or simply hand draw one yourself), as well as photos, pictures, other craft materials (if you want to add dimension). You can look at mandala books for inspirations, designs, and templates. You can also get a mandala coloring book and choose a design that resonates with you and add colors and dimension.

Steps

- Prepare: Outer & Inner Environments.
- Internally, state your intention / make your declaration or claim.
- Example of a declaration: "I Am creating a mandala that invokes what I want to experience regarding my relationship

with money and *money liberation*—as it relates to myself and others."

- On a piece of paper, canvas, or poster board, draw a huge circle.
- Add whatever you would like to your Sacred Circle: pictures, photographs—or create (draw or paint) your own artistic masterpiece.
- Be creative with the area that surrounds your circle.
- Create your own symbolic healing design.
- Invoke your inner child to assist you in this activity.
- Use colors that inspire and delight you.
- Have fun!

North Star Scenarios

As I mentioned previously, at USM I took a course that involved a relationship project and chose God as my relationship focus. To support us in creating an ideal scenario of what we wanted to experience in anything in life—including relationships—we were given paper with a small heart drawn in the center; inside the circle were the words *I Am.* We were instructed to draw spokes that emitted from the heart. On each spoke, we wrote our ideal scenario statements—affirming aspects of what we wanted to experience.

While I had created ideal scenarios prior to my USM experience, after completion of USM's program, creating them became a habit. I continue to use this tool to this day—including within my own *Money Liberation Project.* Sometimes I use spokes on which to write my ideal elements; other times I use balloons and/or flowers and write my affirmations within them. You can create your own way of expressing your North Star scenarios elements using whatever imagery resonates with you.

NOTE: What you write here can also be used when creating your *Money Liberation Project* affirmations, and what you write as your affirmations can also be used to create your North Star scenarios. These scenarios are a more visually creative way of approaching, creating, and energizing your intentions and declaring and claiming statements. Creating a colorful North Star graphic is also an optional step.

Also, you can use the *addendum statement* template (see Vision Creation in Chapter 5) and place that at the bottom of this graphic to help energize your affirmations. More information about affirmations can be found in the next chapter.

Materials Needed

- Paper / Journal
- Crayons, colored pens
- Optional: graphic(s), photograph(s)
- Straight edge to help create spokes (if you so choose)

Steps

- Prepare: Outer & Inner Environments.
- Internally, state your intention / make your declaration or claim.
- Example of a declaration: "I Am creating my North Star scenarios depiction that invokes what I want to experience regarding my relationship with money and *money liberation*—as it relates to me and others."
- Be creative.
- You can invoke your playful inner child to assist you in this activity.
- You can create whatever you would like as your center graphic (where your North Star declarations emit from)—use pictures

or photographs, or create (draw or paint) your own artistic masterpiece.

- Have fun!

My North Star Scenario

My North Star Scenario (cont.)

My North Star Scenario (cont.)

Chapter 5

Your North Star Navigation Guidance System

Prior to diving into any project, big task, meeting, and so on, I take time to create and establish my intentions, declaration affirmations, and vision for what I would like to experience. These tools, I believe, help to establish clear direction of movement, energy, and focus—and can be your inner North Star guidance system.

This chapter will offer guidance and steps to assist you in creating clear, specific, and energy-infused intentions, declarations and claims, affirmations, and vision creation. While the focus relates to your *Money Liberation Project*, these are tools that you can apply to any and every aspect in your life.

Intentions = Energy-Directed Goals

Before I sat down to begin writing *The Energetics of Money Liberation ~ 6 Steps for Finding and Releasing Your Blocks to Experiencing Financial Liberation NOW!* and the PLAY*book*, I followed the protocol within this chapter and began by creating intentions. Here is one of my favorite and most power-filled intentions for my work—particularly my writing.

> *My intention is to experience the expansiveness and freedom of my own personal money liberation, supporting and assisting others in discovering how to connect with and experience* money liberation *for themselves, and sharing vulnerably—through my writing (books, blogs, articles) plus coaching sessions, workshops, podcasts, and videos.*

Intentions do carry energy: the energy in which they are created, the energy in which they are held by the person creating the intention, plus directed energy toward the intended goal.

This energy warrants conscious exploration and, in some cases, adjustments. Energetic adjustments can be made to put something more in alignment, not only with the desired outcome but also in keeping the highest and best benefit for both the intention setter and for those affected by and involved with the intention.

Energetic Qualities of Intentions / Energetically Infused Goals

- Direct positive / affirmative focus
- Commitment to being open and vulnerable
- Commitment to transformation
- Willingness / flexibility / adaptability
- Projection of positive energy and imagining a positive outcome—as if planting seeds—in your future

Creating Money Liberation Project Intentions Support

In many of the transformational programs, courses, and workshops I have taken since the 1980s, the following success mindset left an impression on me. Though various people and organizations state it in different ways, here is the central idea:

> *If this ________________ (book, program, project) were to be ________________ (immensely, wildly, greatly) successful, what would you experience?*

Now, it is your turn. Answer the following:

> *If this ________________ (book, program, project) were to be ________________ (immensely, wildly, greatly) successful, I would experience ________________.*

Before going within, with your thinking-mind, make notes of the type of things you think you want to experience—and state them in an affirmative way. An example of an *affirmative way* means instead of stating "*not* being as confused" (what you *don't* want and using the word *not*)—state *clarity* (what you *do* want).

Another example: Instead of stating "*not* being so disconnected / distant from money and financial prosperity"—state "experiencing connection with money and financial prosperity." List anything that comes to mind. Journal your responses in the space provided below.

My thinking-mind response: What I want to experience is ...

Journal (cont.)

While you most likely answered the query easily and off the top of your head (from your thinking-mind), now go within and seek a deeper answer (one that comes from your Heart and Soul). Journal your response.

My deeper level response: What I want to experience is ...

Journal (cont.)

Intentions

Using *The Energetics of Money Liberation* book and this PLAY*book* as examples of a subject for my intentions, after going within, my deep level responses were:

If *The Energetics of Money Liberation* book and PLAY*book* were to be *amazingly* and *wildly* successful, I would experience:

- inner joy;
- greater inner peace;
- a sense of greater financial safety and security;
- joy and gratitude in knowing that I assisted others in an improved perception of their relationship with money;
- excitement in witnessing their healing, boon in confidence, and expanded finances in which to enjoy, share, and support heart- and soul-connected causes and organizations;
- an enhanced perception of an ever-improving and ever-increasing expansion and deepening of my own perception of my relationship with money in which I can enjoy, share, and support my heart- and soul-connected causes and organizations; and/or
- being of service.
- an expansion of my personal, intimate experience of the True Nature of Spirit—joyfully and giving abundantly of all of the riches of God's Kingdom—including money.

NOTE: After going within, here is what came forward as some of my energy-directed intentions:

My intentions are to

- share what I have learned, developed, and provided within *The Energetics of Money Liberation* and the PLAY*book* with others;
- assist in the spreading of the loving spirit of philanthropy;
- become a full-time philanthropist;

- assist others in becoming full-time philanthropists; and
- make a positive impact in the lives of others—including my family and friends, communities in which I live and serve within, the nation, and ultimately—our planet.

Going within to Discover Your *Money Liberation* Intention(s)

Regardless of what your mind / mind influencing your body / mind as your body is telling you, it is important to set an intention within and simply trust the process.

Steps

- Prepare: Outer & Inner Environments.
- Set your session intention.
- Example: "My intention is to go within and discover my intention(s) for my *Money Liberation Project*."
- Journal your responses below.

My *Money Liberation Project* Intention(s):

Journal (cont.)

Optional: Journal Queries

After journaling about your intentions, you can also journal as much as you would like regarding your experience of your intention-setting session, impressions, discoveries, lessons learned, insights, epiphanies, surprises, musings ...

Some questions to consider answering or writing about:

- *Did you note similar responses from your initial thinking-mind and after going within? Different responses?*
- *Did any of the responses surprise you?*

You can journal your responses below.

Journal (cont.)

Journal (cont.)

Super-Charging Using "Declaring and Claiming"

If you were to imagine, on a scale of 1 to 10 (with 10 being the highest and 1 being the lowest), the power behind intentions (or what I like to call *oomph*) compared to declaring and claiming:

Intentions = 5   Declaring and Claiming = 10

The differences—as I view and have experienced them—between intentions, declaring and claiming, and affirmations, are the following:

- Intentions: sowing seeds on the ground
- Declaring and Claiming: digging in the soil and actually planting the seeds consciously
- Affirmations: watering, cultivating, and nurturing the seeds

Energetic Qualities of Declaring and Claiming

- Being positive / supportive / powerful / strong / affirming
- Being bold
- Expansiveness
- Elevating your consciousness by reaching higher and higher
- Unwavering certainty
- Conviction
- Clarity
- A sense of excitement / delight / FUN!
- Grounding in the here and now
- Projection of positive energy *now* and the image of successful outcomes propelling you into your future

Examples of Declaring and Claiming

- I am experiencing *money liberation now!*
- Vast sums of money are gravitating to me *now*!
- I *love* sharing my wealth with organizations and programs that are important to me!

- *Money liberation* is here for me—right now!
- As a daughter / son of the Most High, I am inherently worthy of receiving financial prosperity *now*!
- As a daughter / son of the Divine, I am claiming my birth-right—prosperity on all levels—including money.
- Right here and right now, I am on my *money liberation* path.

Going within to Discover Your *Money Liberation* Declaring and Claiming Statements

As always, regardless of what your mind / mind influencing your body / mind as your body is telling you, it is important to set an intention within and simply trust the process.

Steps

- Prepare: Outer & Inner Environments
- Set your session intention—and/or practice declaring and claiming. Examples:
    - Intention: "My intention is to go within and discover my declaration and claiming statements for my *Money Liberation Project*."
    - Declaring and Claiming: "I am making my declaration and claiming statements about my *Money Liberation Project*."
- Journal your responses below.

Journal (cont.)

Journal (cont.)

Affirmations

Intentions plus declaring and claiming can be a springboard for affirmations.

Affirmations are positive and supportive declarative statements. The purpose of using affirmations is to anchor or ground the positive energy of your intentions and/or declaring and claiming statements in the present and catapult them into the future. Additionally, by using some specific wording, your affirmations can support greater energetic alignment with your intentions and declaring and claiming.

There is a huge energetic difference between wishful thinking and affirmations. Wishful thinking begins with phrases such as *I want to, I hope to, It would be nice if,* and so on. The energy with these types of statements is wistful, weak, and tentative, and leaves room for ambiguity and doubt. Those types of words imply a longing and pining for something to happen. Those words also leave a lot of space for the energy of something *not* to happen because the implied energy is, "It would be nice if happens, *but* ..."

Every time the word or even the unconscious (subconscious) and/or conscious energy of *but* is used in intentions, declaring and claiming, affirmations, and visioning, you create conflicting and/or competing energy. Conflicting and competing energy negates affirmations. You do not want to leave any invitation for conflicting energy when creating affirmations—or any other kind of positive imagery work.

To create energetically strong affirmations, some specific wording can be beneficial. I found the following helpful when creating my affirmations:

- Begin each sentence with "I Am." This is done to call forward the God / Spirit / Highest Power Within and align it with the God / Spirit / Highest Power Throughout. It also supports being in the here and now.

- State the action word or verb in the present / present-progressive tense (using verbs that end with *–ing,* such as enjoying, playing, dancing). This supports anchoring the energy in the here and now and paves the way, energetically, for your future.

Another key element of affirmations is to keep them somewhat within the realm of possibility for you—at least halfway or, as some workshops, conferences, and training programs suggest, 50 percent or more believable to you. For example, "I Am graduating from medical school with honors" would not be an appropriate or fitting affirmation for me because I have no aptitude to become a medical doctor and am squeamish at the sight of blood. That affirmation is *not* within the realm of possibility nor is it even remotely believable for me.

Having said that, I do believe in miracles. I always avail myself to being open and receptive for miracles within my life at all times. I feel it is important for you to do the same.

Energetic Qualities of Affirmations

- Being positive / supportive / uplifting / affirming
- Commitment to transforming
- Openness / willingness / flexibility / adaptability
- Creation with "as if" energy—envisioning and stating something as though it is already happening here and now to "ground" it as if planting seeds
- Grounds positive energy in the present
- Projection of positive energy and imagining a positive outcome in your future
- Propels positive energy into the future

Examples of Affirmations

- "I Am open and receptive to transforming my relationship with money in an easy and gentle manner."
- "I Am discovering amazing new ways to relate with money—and am experiencing transformational results!"
- "I Am enjoying sharing my abundant financial resources with organizations and causes I care deeply about."
- "I Am enjoying a joy-filled, playful, supportive relationship with money.
- "I Am loving being in the flow with financial prosperity."
- "I Am grateful as I am experiencing the beauty and honor of being a philanthropist—sharing my financial resources with others."

NOTE: What you write below can also be used when creating your ideal scenario (see previous chapter) because ideal scenarios are filled with your affirmations. As mentioned in the previous chapter, creating ideal scenarios is optional and it is a visually creative way of approaching, creating, and energizing affirmations. However, taking time to follow the points explained in this segment on affirmations, I believe, is vital and foundationally imperative for the success of your project. Laying this groundwork was important for me and for the success of my *Money Liberation Project*.

Now it is time for you to create your *money liberation* affirmations.

- I Am

- I Am

- I Am

- I Am

Addendum Statements

It is always a good idea to keep yourself open and flexible. While you may envision one thing, God / Spirit / Your Highest Power may have something in mind even greater and grander than you could ever conceive of and/or imagine.

Again, I do believe in miracles, and I want to be open and receptive to them at all times. That is why I like to include a supportive addendum at the end of my intentions, declaring and claiming statements, affirmations, ideal scenarios, and vision stories.

Some training programs I have attended use various addendum statements to intentions and affirmations—or none at all. I like to use them because it allows more "wiggle-room" for Spirit to work Spirit's magic.

Energetic Qualities of Addendum Statements

- Openness
- Receptiveness
- Expansiveness
- Flexibility
- Possibility

Below is a template you can use to create your own addendum statement.

> *I (embrace / claim / affirm) this, or something even more (grand / magnificent / delightful), for the (greatest / maximum / highest / grandest) (benefit / blessing / outcome) for myself and all others.*

Now create your own addendum statement. Journal your response here.

Journal (cont.)

Vision Creation

I define a *vision creation* as affirmations that are compiled in a way that creates a positive energetic response within. I view it as a trade-in and upgrade from one's old victim story. Your vision creation can be a list of affirmations or a narrative. You can add color, pictures, or anything you can think of that will enhance the positive energy you are consciously creating. (See **Example of a Vision Creation** below.)

Energetic Qualities of Vision Stories

- Being positive / supportive / uplifting / affirming / enthusiastic
- Commitment to transforming
- Openness / willingness / flexibility / adaptability
- Creation with "as if" energy—envisioning and stating something as though it is already happening here and now to "ground" it as if planting seeds
- Grounds positive energy in the present
- Projection of positive energy and imagining a positive outcome in your future
- Propels positive energy into the future
- Multisensory imagery

Example of a Vision Creation

I'm excited! I Am experiencing an amazing relationship with money! I Am open and receptive to experiencing God's Love for me—which includes being financially prosperous. As a daughter of the Most High, I Am claiming my birthright—and I am entitled to experience miracles—including a miraculous transformation in my relationship and experience with money. I Am guided and sustained by God's Love—and resources—including financial resources. I Am being supported and guided. God adores me. I Am feeling secure knowing and experiencing God's Love—and support on all levels and departments in my life—including finances—as real!

Each and every day, my relationship with money is transforming into a supportive, fun, exciting and joy-filled experience. I experience more relaxation, calm, and gratitude when I think about my money liberation.

I affirm all of this and even more—much greater, more delightful, and more amazing than what I could ever possibly imagine—for the maximum benefit for myself, others, and the entire planet.

Now it is time for you to create your vision. Journal using the space below.

Journal (cont.)

Journal (cont.)

Journal (cont.)

I ____________________ (embrace/claim/affirm) this, or something even more ______________ (grand/magnificent/delightful), for the ______________________ (greatest/maximum/highest/grandest) __________________ (benefit/blessing/outcome) for myself and all others.

Chapter 6

Divining

I consider the tool of divining to be my personal and portable lie detector. Like a lie detector, it discerns truth / resonance and falsehood / dissonance. Additionally, divining is a tool that can be used to discover and discern energetic blocks and imbalances that are present within your subconscious / unconscious and your energy field.

In the context of both the "GOD Project" and the *Money Liberation Project*, divining is used to discover what negative and/or challenging beliefs / programs, blocks, and imbalances are present that contribute to a perceived "distance" between you and God. Additionally, you can use divining techniques to discover which positive beliefs / programs are missing and contributing to your perception of not experiencing your desired positive relationship with God, money—and other things as well.

It is important to understand that divining your way into your subconscious / unconscious is intended to be a process that is gentle, supportive, and guided by God / Spirit / Highest Power. It is a way to connect the aspect of God Within to that of God Throughout. There are "check-ins" after each and every step along the way to make sure you can proceed without any major disruptive upheaval—on any and all levels. It is important to follow the detailed protocols to make sure this is not, in any way, a disruptive process.

Groundwork: Establish a Baseline

Establishing a baseline is an essential process for each and every divining session. With divining, a baseline of resonance (truth) and dissonance (falsehood) can be discerned. They are also the first things that must be discerned.

Upon questioning, if there is resonance (truth) present, no marked movements of micro muscles are detected; electrical energy flows freely and the muscles will test *strong.* This indicates that there is no disruption or obstruction of the flow of energy and no blocked energy. It is equivalent to getting an affirmative response.

Upon questioning, if there is dissonance (falsehood) present, marked micro muscle movements are detected. This indicates a disruption or obstruction in the flow of electrical energy, resulting in blocked energy and causing the muscles to test *weak*. It is equivalent to getting a not-affirmative response.

After a clear baseline has been established, you can begin testing anything (food, supplement, statement, idea) to see if it is *energetically* congruent / beneficial / present for you and your energy system and presents a *strong* or *yes* response. Additionally, you can decipher whether something is *energetically* incongruent / not beneficial / not present for you and your energy system, resulting in a *weak* or *no* response.

If you are not able to discern your *yes* and *no* response, see ***What to Do if You Are Not Able to Discern Your Yes and No*** on page 79.

Divining Techniques and How to Establish Baselines

There are numerous techniques for divining. In this chapter, I will share some methods that require two people and other methods that you can do by yourself.

While there are more techniques within each method, what I am sharing will provide you with a variety of ways to easily explore, practice, and master divining—either with a partner or by yourself. Detailed steps for each method presented are included. Also included is information regarding what establishing your baselines will look like and what you can expect to experience for each of the divining techniques.

> At any time during the entire process,
>
> 1. Stop if you meet resistance;
> 2. Continue when ready; and again,
> 3. *Always* stop if you meet any resistance at any stage.

Two-Person Divining and Establishing Baselines

The first three techniques are for divining while working with a partner.

Outstretched Arm Divining (Standing or Sitting)

Tester: Begin by having the test taker (testee) outstretch either arm to the side of his or her body.

- Set your intention to clearly and easily establish the testee's *strong* (or *yes*) and *weak* (or *no*) baselines. (See below.)
- If testee is standing, stand in front of the testee's raised arm; if testee is seated, sit in chair in front of the testee's raised arm.
    - You can also stand behind the testee.
    - Whichever you choose, continue testing consistently, using the same procedures throughout.
- Place one hand on the shoulder of the side of the testee's outstretched arm; the other hand should be on the testee's outstretched forearm.
- While divining, do not exert brute force. Lightly apply pressure on the testee's forearm. (This is not a test of anyone's physical force, willpower, and/or resistance strength.)

Testee:

- Set your intention to clearly and easily establish your *strong* (or *yes)* and *weak* (or *no*) baselines.

- Do not exert tense resistance. Use mild resistance. (Again, this is not a test of anyone's willpower, physical strength, and/or resistance strength.)

Establish Your Baselines[2]: Strong or Yes

Goal / Intention: To get a clear response without muscle strain, force, and so on. While divining, the testee's arm position should remain *strong* after stating something that is *true*.

- Testee: With an outstretched arm, say something that is *true* while maintaining mild resistance. For example:
- My name is _______________.
- Tester: Lightly apply pressure on the testee's outstretched forearm.
- Testee: Continue to maintain mild resistance.

Baseline Response: *Strong* or *Yes*. If—while stating something that is true and divining—the testee's arm position remains *strong* and does not release, this would indicate a *yes = truthful / congruent* statement.

The tester and testee can now discern what the testee's *yes / affirmative / congruent* divining response baseline response looks like and feels like.

NOTE: If testee's arm position becomes *weak* (or *no*) when testing a *true* statement or *strong* (or *yes*) when testing a *false* statement, or if you get what you perceive as a lack of any discernible response—stop! Refer to ***What to Do if You Are Not Able to Discern Your Yes and No*** on page 79.[3]

[2] For the remainder of **the PLAY*book***, refer to ***Establish Your Baselines (All Divining Sessions)*** (pp. 78–79) for the steps regarding establishing a clear *strong* or *yes* response and a clear *weak* or *no* response when divining. See individual methods for how each *strong* or *yes* and *weak* or *no* will look and feel.

[3] Always refer to ***What to Do if You Are Not Able to Discern Your Yes and No*** on p. 79 if you cannot discern responses.

After every step:

Divining Continuation Protocol[4]
(Two-Person or One-Person Methods)

- Divine if you can proceed.
- If testee's arm / forearm position / finger link / finger position remains *strong* (*yes*), continue.
- If testee's arm / forearm position / finger link / finger position becomes *weak* (*no*), refer to ***What to Do if You Get a No (Weak) to Proceed*** on page 80.

Establish Your Baselines[5]**: Weak or No**

Goal / Intention: To get a clear *weak* or *no* without muscle strain, force, and so on. While divining, the testee's arm hold should become *weak* and essentially collapse its position after stating something *false*.

- Testee: With an outstretched arm, say something that is *not true* while maintaining mild resistance. For example:

  My name is ______________. (State a false name.)

- Tester: Lightly apply pressure on the testee's outstretched forearm.
- Testee: Continue to maintain mild resistance.

Baseline Response: *Weak* or *No*. If—while stating something that is not true and divining—the testee's arm position becomes *weak* and does not remain strong, this would indicate a *no* = *not truthful / incongruent* statement.

---

4 After every step, follow this ***Divining Continuation Protocol***.

5 Reminder: For the remainder of **the PLAY*book***, refer to ***Establish Your Baselines (All Divining Sessions)*** (p. 78–79 for the steps regarding establishing a clear *strong* or *yes* response and clear *weak* or *no* response when divining. See individual methods for how each *strong* or *yes* and *weak* or *no* will look and feel.

The tester and testee have now established what the testee's *no / not affirmative / incongruent* divining baseline looks like and feels like. Additionally, via divining, the tester and testee can now discern between *yes / truthful / congruent* and *no / not truthful / incongruent* responses.

Forearm (Standing or Sitting) Divining

Tester: Begin by having the test taker (testee) either stand up or sit down.

- If testee is standing or sitting in a chair with no armrest, have testee raise the forearm of their choosing along the front side of their body, to a point halfway between their hip and shoulder.
- If testee is sitting in a chair with an armrest, have testee rest their elbow joint bone on the armrest, with the forearm at a 45-degree angle to the armrest.

NOTE: The tester can actually apply light pressure on the forearm in the direction toward the testee's shoulder or on the forearm toward the hip / armrest. Once you use one direction of pressure, keep the direction consistent for the remainder of the session.

Tester and Testee

- Set your intentions to clearly and easily establish the testee's *strong* or *yes* and *weak* or *no* baselines.
- Tester—Do not exert brute force; Testee—Do not exert tense resistance.

Establish Your Baselines — Forearm (Standing or Sitting) Divining

Baseline Response: *Strong* or *Yes*. Regardless of the direction of pressure, if—while stating something that is true and divining—the testee's arm position remains *strong* and does not release, this would indicate a *yes = truthful / congruent* statement.

The tester and testee have now established what the testee's *yes / affirmative / congruent* divining baseline looks like and feels like.

Baseline Response: *Weak* or *No*. Regardless of the direction of pressure, if—while stating something that is not true and divining—the testee's arm position becomes *weak* and does not remain strong, this would indicate a *no = not truthful / incongruent* statement.

The tester and testee have now established what the testee's *no / not affirmative / incongruent* divining baseline looks like and feels like. Additionally, via divining, the tester and testee can now discern between *yes / truthful / congruent* and *no / not truthful / incongruent* responses.

Lying Down (with Outstretched Arm or Forearm)

Tester: Begin by having the test taker (testee) lie down on a flat surface. Leaving the back of the arm and elbow joint bone on the flat surface, have the testee raise a forearm and hand straight up or just raise the forearm up toward the ceiling.

NOTE: As with the ***Forearm (Standing or Sitting)*** technique above, the tester can actually apply light pressure on the forearm in the direction toward the testee's shoulder or on the forearm toward the hip / flat surface. As always, once you use one direction of pressure, keep the direction consistent for the remainder of the session.

Establish Your Baselines — Lying Down (with Outstretched Arm or Forearm)

Baseline Response: *Strong* or *Yes*. Regardless of the direction of pressure, if—while stating something that is true and divining—the testee's arm position remains *strong* and does not release, this would indicate a *yes = truthful / congruent* statement.

The tester and testee can now discern what the testee's *yes / affirmative / congruent* divining baseline response looks like and feels like.

Baseline Response: *Weak* or *No*. Regardless of the direction of pressure, if—while stating something that is not true and divining—the testee's arm position becomes *weak* and does not remain strong, this would indicate a *no = not truthful / incongruent* statement.

The tester and testee have now established what the testee's *no / not affirmative / incongruent* divining baseline looks like and feels like. Additionally, via divining, the tester and testee can now discern between *yes / truthful / congruent* and *no / not truthful / incongruent* responses.

Divining by Yourself and Establishing Baselines

Divining without a partner is another option. You can divine by yourself using one of the following techniques.

Interlocking Fingers

Begin by interlocking your pinkie fingers together. Actually, you can do this with any of your fingers—except for the thumbs. Additionally, you can form interlocking rings with your fingers by interlocking either middle finger and thumbs or index fingers and thumbs.

Establish Your Baselines — Interlocking Fingers

Baseline Responses: *Strong* or *Yes*. Regardless of which fingers you use, if—while stating something truthful and divining—your interlocking fingers' hold / link remains *strong* and does not release (or "break") with mild resistance and gentle pressure, this would indicate a *yes = truthful / congruent* statement.

You can now discern what your *yes / affirmative / congruent* divining response baseline response looks like and feels like.

Baseline Response: *Weak* or *No*. If—while stating something *not truthful*—your interlocking fingers' hold / link becomes *weak* and "breaks" with mild resistance and gentle pressure, this would indicate a *no = not truthful / incongruent* statement.

You have now established what your *no / not affirmative / incongruent* divining baseline looks like and feels like. Additionally, via divining, you can now discern between *yes / truthful / congruent* and *no / not truthful / incongruent* responses.

Index Indicator

Using either hand's index finger, place the same hand's middle finger on top of your index finger. Apply gentle pressure from the middle finger on the top of the index finger, while using mild resistance.

Establish Your Baselines — Index Indicator

Baseline Responses: *Strong or Yes*. Regardless of which hand's fingers you use, if—while stating something that is true and divining—your index finger remains *strong* and does not bend, this would indicate a *yes = truthful / congruent* statement.

You can now discern what your *yes / affirmative / congruent* divining response baseline response looks like and feels like.

Baseline Response: *Weak* or *No*. If—while stating something not truthful and divining—your index finger becomes weak and bends, this would indicate a *no = not truthful / incongruent* statement.

You have now established what your *no / not affirmative / incongruent* divining baseline looks like and feels like. Additionally, via divining, you can now discern between *yes / truthful / congruent* and *no / not truthful / incongruent* responses.

Armrest Press

Using either arm, place your elbow joint bone on the armrest of a chair with your forearm extending across your chest pointing to the other armrest. Apply gentle pressure between the wrist and elbow of the extended forearm. (An alternative: Place your elbow joint bone on the armrest of a chair with your forearm pointing toward the ceiling.)

Establish Your Baselines — Armrest Press

Baseline Response: *Strong* or *Yes*. If—while stating something that is true and divining—the forearm's position remains *strong* and does not bend toward your lap and/or the armrest), this would indicate a *yes = truthful / congruent* statement.

You can now discern what your *yes / affirmative / congruent* divining response baseline response looks like and feels like.

Baseline Response: *Weak* or *No*. If—while stating something *not truthful* and divining—the forearm's position becomes *weak* and bends toward your lap (or the armrest), this would indicate a *no* =

false / incongruent statement.

You have now established what your *no / not affirmative / incongruent* divining baseline looks like and feels like. Additionally, via divining, you can now discern between *yes / truthful / congruent* and *no / not truthful / incongruent* responses.

Rocking

You can start by either standing or sitting still. For beginners, I recommend starting with standing. (Some people believe you should find north and intend for *true* statements to give a northern indication. I, however, believe one gets what they believe, and I do not believe that step is necessary. It never became a necessary factor for me.)

Establish Your Baselines – Rocking

Baseline Responses: *Strong* or *Yes*. If—while stating something that is true and divining—your body (or torso, if sitting) sways *forward*, this would indicate a *yes = truthful / congruent* statement.

You can now discern what your *yes / affirmative / congruent* divining response baseline response looks like and feels like.

Baseline Response: *Weak* or *No*. If—while stating something *not truthful* and divining—your body (or torso, if sitting) sways *backward*, this would indicate a *no = false / incongruent* statement.

You have now established what your *no / not affirmative / incongruent* divining baseline looks like and feels like. Additionally, via divining, you can now discern between *yes / truthful / congruent* and *no / not truthful / incongruent* responses.

Pendulum

Another way of discerning a *yes / congruent* from a *no / incongruent* via divining is by using a pendulum.

A pendulum can be any weighted object at the end of a string or chain. It can be used as a divining tool to detect micro muscle movements and vibrations, which affects the directional swinging of a pendulum.

Sometimes mastering this technique can take a while. Mastery requires your commitment and/or intention to acquire proficiency, time, focus, and practice.

Important: It is not the pendulum "saying" *yes* or *no*—and it is never meant to be approached in a "go ask the pendulum" manner. A pendulum is simply a means or an instrument, like the lie detector, that can assist you in reading your own energy field via divining.

> Do not confuse the pendulum or the use of a pendulum—while divining in a transformational context—with a Ouija Board. Ouija Boards, and the energy "invoked" and transmitted while using one, and divining with a pendulum as a tool to discern what is energetically congruent or incongruent, are *not* the same thing. In my opinion, the Ouija Board is a gateway for negative / darker energies—and I do not want to invite that kind of energy into my life and energy field.

How to Divine Using a Pendulum

For Beginners ...

Important: If you get an indication to use the pendulum during your *Money Liberation Project*, it is imperative that you first master getting and discerning your clear *yes / congruent* and clear *no / incongruent* responses.

Goal / Intention: To get a clear indication of what your *yes / congruent* and *no / incongruent* responses look like and feel like while divining with a pendulum.

- With the pendulum in front of you, hold the top of the chain (the end away from the weighted object) between your index finger and thumb or between your index and middle fingers. Make sure there is room for the weighted object to swing.

NOTE: The vibration of *yes / congru*ent will move the pendulum one direction while the vibration of *no / incongruent* will move the pendulum in an opposite direction.

Examples:

- A *yes / congruent* response could be an up / down (north / south) movement—the same as a head nodding *yes*.
- A *no / incongruent* response could be a left / right (east / west) movement—the same as a head movement of *no*.

Or ...

- A *yes / congruent* response could be a clockwise movement of the pendulum.
- A *no / incongruent* response could be a counterclockwise movement of the pendulum.

Remember: Be open to whatever movement comes forward for you.

Pendulum Divining Practice Techniques

- Set your intention to clearly and easily establish what your *yes / true / congruent* pendulum direction looks like and feels like.
  - Think or say out loud: "Yes! Yes! Yes!"
  - See which way the pendulum moves (up or down; left or right; circle to the left; circle to the right; and so on). The direction of this movement indicates a *yes = true / congruent* response.
- Set your intention to clearly and easily establish what your *no / false / incongruent* pendulum direction looks like and feels like.
  - Think or say out loud: "No! No! No!"
  - The pendulum should move in the opposite direction of your established *yes* response. The direction of this movement indicates a *no = false / incongruent* response.

NOTE: While you may notice little to no movement, be patient with yourself and your process—and keep practicing.

Pendulum Divining

With the pendulum in front of you, hold the top of the chain (the end away from the weighted object) between your index finger and thumb or index and middle fingers. Make sure there is room for the weighted object to swing.

Establish Your Baselines—Pendulum Divining

Baseline Response: *Strong* or *Yes*. If—while stating something that is true and divining—the pendulum moves in your established *yes* directional movement, this would indicate a *yes = truthful / congruent* statement.

You can now discern what your *yes / true / congruent* divining response baseline response looks like and feels like.

Baseline Response: *Weak* or *No*. If—while stating something *not truthful* and divining—the pendulum moves in your established *no* directional movement, this would indicate a *no = false / incongruent* statement.

You have now established what your *no / false / incongruent* divining baseline looks like and feels like. Additionally, via divining, you can now discern between *yes / truthful / congruent* and *no / not truthful / incongruent* responses.

NOTE: Though not a requirement, meditation is an essential tool to have and to incorporate into one's *Spiritual Tool Kit*. I have found that meditating either before or after any type of divining session has been extremely beneficial for me.

My Pendulum Experience

Initially, I had a challenging time getting a clear *yes* and *no* with a pendulum. I have noticed the same challenge with some of my friends and clients. Upon exploration, I divined, using other techniques, that I (and those who were similarly challenged) had subconscious programs regarding this type of divining as evil, ungodly, and so on. After clearing these subconscious programs and with much practice establishing a baseline with the pendulum, I am happy to report that I (and others I support) now can easily discern *yes* and *no* by using a pendulum. The pendulum is now one of the major go-to techniques I use with myself and with others.

Summary of Divining Steps with Protocols

Below you will find all of the recommended steps and protocols that will assist you with the divining process during your *Money Liberation Project*.

Beginning Session Protocol for All Divining Sessions

For this to be a process of ease and gentleness, it is imperative to establish and adhere to a certain protocol for each and every divining session.

- Prepare: Outer & Inner Environments.
- Invoke God / Spirit / Highest Power and say a heartfelt prayer.
- State your clearing and release intention / declaration and claiming statement (verbally or silently).
- Discern which divining method to use by using your intuition and/or your level of comfort.
- Establish your baselines.

Establish Your Baselines – All Divining Sessions

- State your intention / declaring and claiming statement—to discern, with ease and clarity, your divining baselines.
- Establish your *strong / yes / congruent* baseline.
    - State something that is *true / factual*. Divine.
        - If you test *strong* or *yes*, you have established what your *yes / true / congruent* statement looks like and feels like while divining.
        - If you get test *weak* or *no* when testing the *true / factual* statement—stop!
        - Refer to ***What to Do if You Are Not Able to Discern Your Yes and No*** (next page).
- Establish your *weak / no / incongruent* baseline.

- State something that is *not true*. Divine.
- If you test *weak* or *no* regarding this *not truthful* statement,
    - You have established your *no / false / incongruent* baseline; and
    - You can now discern how your *yes* and *no* feels like and looks like when divining.
- If you are not able to discern between your *yes* and *no*—stop!
    - Refer to ***What to Do if You Are Not Able to Discern Your Yes and No*** (below).

What to Do if You Are Not Able to Discern Your Yes and No

- Drink water. Wait a few minutes and try again.
- Set your intention to experience clarity with discerning *yes* and *no* while divining, in service to your growth, healing, and upliftment.
- This time, think or say out loud: "Yes! Yes! Yes! Yes!" Test for a *yes* baseline. Confirm by stating a true statement. You should experience the same baseline results.
- Now think or say out loud: "No! No! No! No!" Test for a *no* baseline. Confirm by stating a false statement. You should experience the same baseline results.
- Practice, and be patient with yourself.

Divining Continuation Protocol

- Divine if you can proceed.
    - If you test *strong* or *yes*, continue.
    - Ask if you are able to clear and release something at this time. Divine.
        - If you get a *yes* (*strong*), proceed.
        - If you get a *no* (*weak*)—stop!

        - Refer to ***What to Do if You Get a No (Weak) to Proceed*** (see below).

What to Do if You Get a No (Weak) to Proceed[6]

- Drink a glass of water.
- After waiting a few minutes, try again.
    - If you still get a *no* (*weak*), try again another day.
    - Do not continue until you get a *yes* (*strong*) response.
- Additionally, consider
    - going within;
    - praying for clarity and for assistance from God / Spirit / Highest Power;
    - restating your healing intention;
    - being patient and gentle with yourself; and
    - persisting ... another day.

Divining Which Statement to Clear First ... Next ... Next ...

Using divining testing, discern which statement to energetically address, clear, and release first, next, and so on.

Divining Statements Protocol

- Follow the ***Beginning Session Protocol for All Divining Sessions*** (see page 78).
- Referring to the statement charts in Chapter 10, ask God / Spirit / Highest Power which statement to clear first and discern via divining:
    - Lack of Positive Statements: Y/N?
    - Negative / Challenged Statements: Y/N?

[6] From now on, if after getting repeated *no* (*weak*) responses to your correct name when attempting to establish your baseline, whether to proceed, or that a clearing took place—stop. Refer to ***What to Do if You Get a No (Weak) to Proceed.***

- Within the category indicated, ask God / Spirit / Highest Power which of the follow to clear first and discern via divining:
    - Group: A (Y/N?), B (Y/N?), C (Y/N?)
    - Number: 1 (Y/N?), 2 (Y/N?), 3 (Y/N?), 4 (Y/N?), 5 (Y/N?)
- Check the "Challenged" box corresponding to the statement indicated.
- Divine to see if more information is needed (see below for ***Divining for More Information*** and ***Divining for More Information Protocol on*** page 83).
    - Reminder: If you are prompted to divine for more information and if there is an indication that the energetic statement was inherited, you can choose to do one of the following within the statement's *Challenged* box:
        - Circle the check.
        - Place an asterisk or the initial "I" next to the check.
        - Create a way to designate the statement as inherited within the *Challenged* box.
- If, after divining, you are given a go-ahead to proceed, begin Step 5 (see page 219).

NOTE: Within one divining statements session, you may move back and forth between both Negative / Challenged and Lack of Positive statements. (Additionally, when the time comes to do the clearing and release process, there may be times when you will be able to clear and release multiple energetic statements; other times you will only clear and release one or two.)

Be patient with yourself and your process.

Divining for More Information

There were times during my own *Money Liberation Project* that I intuitively sensed I needed to know more about the origin of the experience that caused the block or imbalance. At those times, I would ask God / Spirit / Highest Power something akin to this:

Is there any detail / specific / additional information I need to know about this?

If I received a *strong* or *yes* indication during divining, I would ask Spirit to reveal to me what I needed to know.

Too Much Information or Need to Know?

There were other times that, although I may have been curious about the details surrounding a block and/or imbalance, no additional information was indicated or required for me (and subsequently for my clients) to know in order for the clearing and releasing to take place.

I believe this is the reason: Some people may be quite "head-y." (At times, I tend to be very immersed within my own head.) Some may still want to be attached to their victim story. Their thinking / ego mind wants a bone to chew on; this *munching mind* wants something to gnaw on. Many times, when I ask God / Spirit / Highest Power if I (or my clients) need to know any additional or detailed information, I receive a *no* when divining.

I view receiving a *no* as a directive from God / Spirit / Highest Power and believe there are several reasons for this. It supports an easy and gentle rebalancing by:

- Creating separation from one's *victim* story if one is "head-y";
- Not feeding a munching mind;
- Attempting to prevent picking at and revisiting any former wound(s)—which only serves to uphold or perhaps reactivate the vibration of the wound or wounds, or both; and
- Allowing for whatever was cleared and released to remain cleared and released.

Divining for More Information Protocol

- Ask: *Do I need to know more information about this (in the context of the statement you are focusing on) at this time?* Divine.
- If you receive a *no* response about needing to know additional information, proceed to the protocols for the clearing modality indicated.
- If you receive a *yes* response,
    - Ask something like *"What information do I need to know at this time?"*
    - Use your intuition to be open to information to appear to you in the form of signs, symbols, words, colors, sounds, the experience of emotions, and so on.
- Ask if the issue was inherited.
    - If you get a *yes*, ask: *"What information do I need to know at this time?"* For example: maternal or paternal side? Male or female?
    - Use your intuition to be open to information to appear to you in the form of signs, symbols, words, colors, sounds, the experience of emotions, and so on.
    - Make a notation on the chart's *Challenged* box of an inherited energetic.

PART II

YOUR *MONEY LIBERATION PROJECT*

Chapter 7

Step 1: Evaluate and Determine

Before beginning any transformational program, I believe it is a good practice to evaluate where you are now and where you want to be. The information gleaned from this process will provide you information of your before, during, and after *Money Liberation Project* progress. This information will be helpful to refer back to witness how much progress and transformation has actually taken place at any given time along the way.

If you have already written your responses in Chapter 5, you can:

- Leave your answers in Chapter 5 and complete the portions of this step that you have not yet done;
- Copy your previous responses and insert them here to keep your project contained to one area for easy reference; or
- Update and refine your initial responses by doing them again and notating them in this section.

Evaluate

Start by using the following as the baseline question and journal your responses using the space provided:

When you think about money and how you perceive your relationship with money, generally, how do you feel?

Journal

Journal (cont.)

At this moment, how do you perceive your relationship with money? Journal your response.

Describe your perceived stress or level of challenge now. Journal your response.

Stress / Challenge Evaluation

Find a quiet time and space. Take a moment to consciously and energetically connect with your body through deep breathing. Connect with your feelings. Silently read the questions below. Journal your responses.

On a scale of 1 to 10 (1 = ever so slightly stressed / challenged; 10 = deeply, disturbingly stressed / challenged), rate the following:

_____ *How much of a challenge is / how much stress are you currently experiencing with your perceived relationship with money?*

_____ *When you think about the current status of your relationship with money, what amount of stress do you experience within?*

_____ *How blocked / closed off do you feel regarding your relationship with money?*

_____ *How blocked / closed off do you feel regarding receiving money?*

_____ *How blocked / closed off do you feel regarding sharing your money with others?*

_____ *How much frustration do you feel regarding your relationship with money?*

_____ *How much shame do you feel regarding your perceived current state of your financial resources and/or relationship with money?*

_____ *How hopeless do you feel regarding the "improvement" of this situation / relationship?*

Add other questions, comments, and/or observations about your stresses and challenges. Journal your responses here.

Journal (cont.)

Journal (cont.)

Determine What You Want to Experience

With any project or experiment, it is always a good idea to establish what direction you want to be going in—what you are working toward. A powerful tool to use to help set your energetic direction is to consciously establish what your intentions (energetically infused goals) are for your *Money Liberation Project*. For example, you can establish intentions for the experience of the project, desired end results, the improved quality of the relationship you are seeking, and so on.

Going Within to Discover Your *Money Liberation Project* Intentions

- Prepare: Outer & Inner Environments.
- Set your session intention. Key at this time is setting an intention to connect within, and simply trusting the process, regardless of what your mind / mind influencing your body (your mind as your body) is telling you.

  Example: My intention is to go within and discover the answer to the following question: *If my Money Liberation Project were to be ______________ (immensely, wildly, greatly) successful, I want to experience ...*
- Journal your responses.

Journal (cont.)

Based on what you wrote, create clear and concise intention statements for your key project. Journal your responses.

My intention is to ...

My intention is to ...

My intention is to ...

My intention is to ...

My intention is to ...

- Upon emerging from this session, journal as much as you would like about your experience of your session, discoveries, lessons learned, takeaways, insights, epiphanies, surprises, musings ...
- Additionally, here are some questions to consider answering or journaling about:
    - Did any of your responses surprise you?
    - Upon reflection, if another intention comes forward for you, write it down.
    - If, after reading your intentions, they do not have any "juicy," power-filled energy for you, consider rewriting them until they do.

Journal

Journal (cont.)

Journal (cont.)

Declaring and Claiming

Now add more powerful fuel to your intention with supportive, bold declaring and claiming statements.

- Prepare: Outer & Inner Environments
- Set your session intention—and/or practice declaring and claiming.
  - Examples:
    - Intention: "My intention is to go within and discover my declaration and claiming statements for my *Money Liberation Project*."
    - *Declaring and Claiming*: "I am making my declaration and claiming statements about my *Money Liberation Project* now!"
- Journal your responses below.

Journal (cont.)

Journal (cont.)

Affirmations

Using your intentions and declaring and claiming statements, create your *Money Liberation Project* affirmations.

- Prepare: Outer & Inner Environments
- Set your session intention.
    - Example: My intention is to go within and create *Money Liberation Project* affirmations.
- Journal your responses.

Journal (cont.)

Journal (cont.)

Create Your Vision and Start Creating Your New Money Story

Using your affirmations above, create your vision for your *Money Liberation Project*—and what your new "money story" will be like.

- Prepare: Outer & Inner Environments
- Set your session intention.
  - Example: My intention is to go within and create my vision for my *Money Liberation Project* and for my new relationship with money.
- Journal your responses.

Journal (cont.)

Journal (cont.)

Journal (cont.)

I ____________________ (embrace / claim / affirm) this, or something even more __________________ (grand/magnificent/delightful), for the ________________________ (greatest/maximum/highest/grandest) ______________________ (benefit/blessing/outcome) for myself and all others.[7]

[7] This statement can also be used after your intentions, declaring and claiming, affirmations, and ideal scenarios.

Chapter 8

Step 2: Explore

I believe it is imperative to consciously explore your memory to trace the root cause of your sense and perception of separation from money / financial prosperity / *money liberation*: what you learned about money, how you learned it, and from whom.

In this section, you will examine your indoctrinations, perceptions, characteristics of your most challenging parental figure, and discover which of the same challenging characteristics you may have projected onto your perception of and experience with money.

Indoctrinations about Money

Whether you realized it or not, you were indoctrinated by a variety of sources as you were growing up. First, you'll look at your religious influences and then your religious influences from your family of origin. After considering each statement, journal your responses.

Religion / Church Indoctrination

How was money and having money described in books, songs, and movies you were exposed to while growing up? How were wealthy people described? Journal your response.

Journal (cont.)

How were you described in relation to money? (Example: not being worthy? Best to be separated from money because money / having money was sinful? and so on.) Journal your responses.

Family of Origin Indoctrination

If your mother was present during your upbringing, how did she describe money / having or not having money / wealthy people? (If your mother was not present, how did the most influential female figure in your life while growing up describe money / having or not having money / wealthy people?) What judgments were made? Journal your responses.

If your father was present during your upbringing, how did he describe money / having or not having money / wealthy people? (If your father was not present, how did the most influential male figure in your life describe money / having or not having money / wealthy people while you were growing up?) What judgments were made? Journal your responses.

Perceptions of Relationships with Money

The ways in which your parental influences related to money / those with money, and so on—as well as your perceptions of their relationships with money—affected your perception of your own relationship with money. In this next section, you will consider those influences and journal your thoughts about them.

Perceptions of Parental Figures' Relationships with Money

If you were to describe the relationship your mother (or the most influential female in your life while growing up) had with money—based purely on your perspective and perceptions—how would you describe it? Journal your responses.

If you were to describe the relationship your father (or the most influential male in your life while growing up) had with money—based purely on your perspective and perceptions—how would you describe it? Journal your responses.

Perceptions of Your Relationship with Money

If you were to describe your relationship with money while you were growing up—based purely on your perspective and perceptions—how would you describe it? Journal your responses.

Today, if you were to describe your relationship with money—based purely on your perspective and perceptions—how would you describe it? Any judgments? Journal your responses.

Looking back, in what ways did your relationship with money reflect and resemble your relationship with your most challenging parental figure? Journal your responses.

Challenging Characteristics and Relationships

Challenging relationship characteristics can be repeated and experienced in multiple relationships—including your relationship with money. Explore the challenging common denominator(s) within your relationships—in general. Journal your responses.

Journal (cont.)

Challenging Parental Figure

Which relationship did you find to be more challenging while you were growing up: the relationship with your mother (or an influential female figure) or with your father (or an influential male figure)? Answer here.

How would you describe the characteristics of the person you were more challenged by? Journal your responses.

Journal (cont.)

Challenging Figure

Does your most challenging parental figure or influential person possess the same characteristics that you attribute to money? (Example: aloof, distant, and so on.) Answer here.

According to your experience, opinion, perceptions, and perspectives, what do your most challenging figure and money have in common? Journal your responses.

Journal (cont.)

Challenging Relationships

Reflecting on your most challenging relationships, what did / do they have in common with your most challenging parental figure or influential person? Journal your responses.

According to your experience, opinion, perceptions, and perspectives, what did / do your most challenging relationships and money have in common? Journal your responses.

Journal (cont.)

Journal (cont.)

We are in relation to everything—including money—at all times. How would you describe your relationship with money now? Journal your responses.

Journal (cont.)

Now—set your North Star to where you want it to be regarding your relationship with money. Journal your responses.

Journal (cont.)

Journal (cont.)

Chapter 9

Step 3: Examine Your Thoughts and Feelings

In this next step, you will examine thoughts and feelings that contributed to the creation and perpetuation of your story of your relationship with money. Go within, and be as honest as possible. Journal what comes forward for you as you read through the following ideas.

When answering these questions, you can use paper separate from your journal in case you would like to shred these pages after your clearing and releasing.

Judgments and Resentments

What judgments / resentments—if any—do you hold against your most challenging parent / influential person—specifically as it relates to money / finances? Journal your responses.

Journal (cont.)

Journal (cont.)

What judgments / resentments do you hold about not being where you want to be financially? Who do you hold these judgments / resentments against? Journal your responses.

Journal (cont.)

Journal (cont.)

What judgments do you hold against yourself as they relate to your relationship with money? Examples: "I am a poor sinner—and I will always be poor"; "I am not working hard enough"; "It is my lot in life to be struggling and not rich"; and so on. Journal your responses.

Journal (cont.)

Journal (cont.)

What—if any—judgments / resentments do you think your family and friends might experience—or what would they say about you if you were "rich"? Journal your responses.

Journal (cont.)

How do you think your relationship with others would change if you had a lot of money? What—if any—judgments / resentments would you hold against others if you were "rich"? Journal your responses.

Journal (cont.)

Relationship Mirrors and Projections

Relationships can act as mirrors of both conscious and subconscious feelings, attitudes, beliefs, perceptions, and misperceptions. Quite often, what we do not want to accept in ourselves, we project (or place) onto others—especially things we deem as negative.

Listed below are additional questions to ask yourself and journal about—particularly as they relate to your money personality.

Money—and Your "Shadow" / Fear-Based Side

What do you hope is not true of your money personality—yet most likely is? Journal your response.

Journal (cont.)

What are you most afraid about as it relates to money? Journal your response.

Journal (cont.)

What do you fear about having a lot of money? Journal your response.

Journal (cont.)

Your Money Personality—Getting Supportive Feedback

Ask someone who knows you well and who you trust to honestly to describe your personality as it relates to money. If that is not possible, imagine how someone who knew you well described your personality—as it relates to money / your spending / savings / donating / being money generous or money hoarding, and so on.

Description Notes:

Notes (cont.)

Notes (cont.)

Your Money Personality's Shadow-Side Traits

Now that you have discovered what a trusted person honestly perceives and observes about your money personality, ask yourself what traits you perceive as negative and trigger a defensive response from you. Journal your response.

Journal (cont.)

Journal (cont.)

Your Money Personality's "Light-Side" Traits

What do you perceive are aspects of your positive or "light" side of your personality as it relates to money? Journal your response.

Journal (cont.)

Journal (cont.)

Refer back to how the person you trust described your money personality. (Again, if that was not possible, refer back to someone who knew you well and how that person described your personality.) What traits do / did you perceive as positive and yet trigger / triggered a defensive ("that couldn't possibly be me") response from you? Journal your response.

Journal (cont.)

Journal (cont.)

Other People's Light-Side Money Personality Traits

What money personality characteristics or qualities do you most admire in others—and feel are not true of you? Journal your response.

Journal (cont.)

What admired characteristics or qualities of others' money personalities do you share—and are willing to now embrace? Journal your response.

Journal (cont.)

Journal (cont.)

Imagine This ...

If God / Spirit / Your Highest Power were to have a money personality, describe what it would be like. Journal your response.

Journal (cont.)

Journal (cont.)

Journal (cont.)

What aspects of God's / Spirit's / Your Highest Power's money personality would you like to experience, embrace, and embody more of? Journal your response.

Journal (cont.)

Journal (cont.)

Chapter 10

Step 4: Expose via Divining

In the previous step, you were asked to examine your thoughts and feelings about money, your perceived relationship with money, and your perceived relationship with money, you, and others—including God. Based on what you wrote, you will now be asked to create your own Lack of Positive and Negative / Challenged statements to use for your *Money Liberation Project.* These energetic statements can be used to begin the next step of exposing what needs to be cleared and removed through divining.

Positive and Negative Aspects

As you learned in the main book, I believe a holistic approach to removing blocks and imbalances in the conscious mind and the subconscious involves addressing *both* the presence of Negative / Challenged statement energetics, programs, and vibrations *plus* the Lack of Positive statement energetics, programs, and vibrations.

Statement Lists Format

The format of the statements lists was designed to support easy tracking of the statements. There is no particular statement hierarchy, order, or grouping. Each chart page has the following:

- Type of statement (Lack of Positive or Negative / Challenged)
- Page number
- Fifteen statements broken down into three groups (A, B, C) of five statements (1 through 5) for easy tracking
- A place to note when you were challenged as indicated via divining

  - If you test *weak* or *no* regarding a positive statement on a Lack of Positive Statements chart.
  - If you test *strong* or *yes* regarding a negative statement on a Negative / Challenged Statements chart.
  - If you test *strong* or *yes* for needing to know more information about the energetic.
- A place to notate the energetic was cleared and released

What You Will Be Tracking

During your *Money Liberation Project*, you will be tracking which energetic statement best represents your Challenged Energetics blocks and imbalances—and those that are not a challenge *plus* statement energetics that indicate you need to know more information. You will also be tracking the energetic clearing and release.

Challenged Energetics

Lack of Positive Statements

- While divining, if you get a *strong* or *yes* response to a positive statement, you can leave the *Challenged* box clear or mark the box with a "0." (Leaving the box blank makes it easier to clearly spot the checked boxes.) These statements contain the subconscious / unconscious and conscious thoughts, energy, and vibration that resonate as what you hold as *True*.
- If you get a *weak* or *no* response, mark the *Challenged* box with a check. These statements represent energetic dissonance and what you hold within your subconscious / unconscious and conscious thoughts, energy, and vibration as *False* or *Not True*.

Negative / Challenged Statements

- While divining, if you get a *weak* or *no* response to a negative statement, mark the box with a 0. These statements contain the subconscious / unconscious and conscious thoughts, energy, and vibration that resonate as what you hold as *False or Not True.*

- If you get a *strong* or *yes* response, mark the *Challenged* box with a check. These statements contain the subconscious / unconscious and conscious thoughts, energy, and vibration that resonate as what you hold as *True.*

Need to Know More Information (Any Statement)

- While divining, if you get a *strong* or *yes* response after inquiring if you need to know more information, within the *Challenged* box either add an "I," circle the "check," or create your own notation.

Clearing and Releasing

In Chapter 11, you will learn how to clear and release energetic blocks and imbalances.

Lack of Positive Statements

- When a Lack of Positive Statement energetic clearing and release has taken place, it means that the energetic block and/or imbalance toward resonance with the positive statement and associated energy has been removed.

Negative / Challenged Statements

- When a Negative / Challenged Statements energetic clearing and release has taken place, it means that whatever negative energetic block and/or imbalance which created resonance with the Negative / Challenged Statements within your subconscious / unconscious and/or energy field has been cleared.

Within the *Cleared* box, you can either write the date it was cleared, check the box indicating a clearing, or write a "C".

In the statements lists in this chapter, the first five pages are blank Lack of Positive Statements forms on which you can write your desired positive personal statements. These statements can include what you think, hope, and want to be true of your perception of and relationship with money—and yet may fear might not be true for you. These pages will also assist you in tracking your progress of clearing and releasing energetic blocks and imbalances that have been separating you from experiencing / perceiving a more constructive and supportive relationship with money.

NOTE: After your created statements, additional statements are provided.

The lists I have provided regarding both Lack of Positive Statements and Negative / Challenged Statements are:

- not all-inclusive;
- not in any specific order or hierarchy; and
- merely samplings.

NOTE: You might not want to divine each provided energetic statement—or you may want to divine all of them. I suggest that you divine to discern if it would be beneficial for you to use the provided statements—or not.

Following the Lack of Positive Statements pages, you will find five blank Negative / Challenged Statements forms on which to write your perceived negative and/or challenging perceptions and feelings statements related to money and your perceived relationship with money. This is where you can track your clearing and releasing of negative perceptions and feelings / energetic blocks and imbalances which have also contributed to your perceived / misperceived separation from money, financial prosperity, and *money liberation*.

Again, after your created statements, additional statements are provided.

NOTE: The number of statements, the exact statements, and the kind of statements (Lack of Positive or Negative / Challenged) that need to be cleared vary for each individual. As more layers are revealed and cleared, even more statements and corresponding energetic vibrations may be revealed. As I wrote in *GETTING GOD® ~ "The GOD Project"* and in *The Energetics of Money Liberation*, our perceived challenges can have multiple layers, like an onion, that need to be peeled away one layer at a time.

To get the most transformative value out of this process, it is best to be as vulnerable, open, and honest with yourself as possible. There is no judgment—so go for the greatest amount of healing possible for you at this time.

Remember ...

This is not a mental / thinking / figuring-it-out process. This is not a processing of any "story" process. It involves trusting what is energetically identified by using energy-identifying tools. If you want to use a mind, allow your God Mind—your Divine Mind—to lead this process.

Divining Which Statements to Address

Remember to follow all protocols at all times. In this section, you will focus on:

- Following the ***Beginning Session Protocol for All Divining Sessions*** (see page 78); and
- Following the ***Divining Statements Protocol*** (see pages 80–81).

Remember—you do not have to divine for each and every statement—or you can. You can begin by addressing the statements you created, or you can begin with the statements provided. There is no *wrong* way to approach this. As always, to find the best way for you to approach these statements, go within, ask, and divine to discern which way would work best for you.

NOTE: Though the statements within the Lack of Positive Statements chart are *positive* statements, the intention is to test and track which positive statement energetic is *lacking* or *absent* from one's energy field and/or subconscious.

Lack of Positive Statements (Page 1)	Challenged	Info	Cleared
Group A			
1.			
2.			
3.			
4.			
5.			
Group B			
1.			
2.			
3.			
4.			
5.			
Group C			
1.			
2.			
3.			
4.			
5.			

Lack of Positive Statements (Page 2)	Challenged	Info	Cleared
Group A			
1.			
2.			
3.			
4.			
5.			
Group B			
1.			
2.			
3.			
4.			
5.			
Group C			
1.			
2.			
3.			
4.			
5.			

Lack of Positive Statements (Page 3)	Challenged	Info	Cleared
Group A			
1.			
2.			
3.			
4.			
5.			
Group B			
1.			
2.			
3.			
4.			
5.			
Group C			
1.			
2.			
3.			
4.			
5.			

Lack of Positive Statements (Page 4)	Challenged	Info	Cleared
Group A			
1.			
2.			
3.			
4.			
5.			
Group B			
1.			
2.			
3.			
4.			
5.			
Group C			
1.			
2.			
3.			
4.			
5.			

Lack of Positive Statements (Page 5)	Challenged	Info	Cleared
Group A			
1.			
2.			
3.			
4.			
5.			
Group B			
1.			
2.			
3.			
4.			
5.			
Group C			
1.			
2.			
3.			
4.			
5.			

Lack of Positive Statements (Page 6)	Challenged	Info	Cleared
Group A			
1. Money gravitates to me.			
2. I am a good steward of money.			
3. I am worthy of receiving all that is good—including money.			
4. Money is good.			
5. I deserve to have money.			
Group B			
1. Being rich and wealthy is part of my destiny.			
2. I give myself permission to be rich and financially prosperous.			
3. I give myself permission to be wealthy.			
4. I am ready to accept money liberation—now!			
5. I am willing to accept money liberation—now!			
Group C			
1. I am able to accept money liberation—now!			
2. I give myself permission to experience money liberation—now!			
3. I am open and receptive to becoming rich—now!			
4. I am open and receptive to receiving money—now!			
5. I can be rich—now!			

Lack of Positive Statements (Page 7)	Challenged	Info	Cleared
Group A			
1. I can be wealthy—now!			
2. Money is always there for me.			
3. I trust myself with handling money.			
4. I am excited about all of the good I can do with money.			
5. When I think about my finances, I feel calm.			
Group B			
1. I am comfortable with having a vast sum of money.			
2. I can be trusted with money.			
3. I do not have to struggle to make money.			
4. Money is part of my divine inheritance.			
5. Money liberation and financial prosperity is possible for me.			
Group C			
1. I can have more than I need.			
2. It is okay for me to splurge on luxury items for myself.			
3. It is okay for me to splurge on luxury items for my family and friends.			
4. I am okay with experiencing being rich.			
5. I can spend money on myself.			

Lack of Positive Statements (Page 8)	Challenged	Info	Cleared
Group A			
1. I am good with money.			
2. If money is a game—I can win!			
3. If money is a game—I am winning!			
4. I can do what I love and become rich.			
5. God loves me regardless of my financial status.			
Group B			
1. Money can come to me in various ways.			
2. Working hard is not the only way to become rich.			
3. It is possible for me to change my financial status for the better.			
4. I am capable of changing my financial status for the better.			
5. I can do what I love to do and become rich.			
Group C			
1. What I love to do and how I make money can be the same thing.			
2. I am open and receptive to receiving money from a variety of different venues.			
3. I am open and receptive to change—including changing my finances for the better.			
4. I am open and receptive to learning more about financial management and investing.			
5. I do not have to suffer financially.			

Lack of Positive Statements (Page 9)	Challenged	Info	Cleared
Group A			
1. I do not have to suffer—including financially.			
2. I am destined to experience financial prosperity.			
3. I can be a financially successful artist.			
4. I am a financially successful artist.			
5. Money flows to me.			
Group B			
1. Money gravitates to me like a magnet.			
2. There is plenty of money to go around—including for me!			
3. I can live lavishly.			
4. I am worthy of living lavishly.			
5. It is okay for me to be rich.			
Group C			
1. It is okay for me to be wealthy.			
2. I can be a giving philanthropist.			
3. I am a generous giver—including donating money.			
4. I am capable of becoming a generous giver—including giving money.			
5. I am responsible with my money.			

Lack of Positive Statements (Page 10)	Challenged	Info	Cleared
Group A			
1. I make wise financial choices and decisions.			
2. Regardless of my financial status, I can still have a close relationship with God.			
3. I can be safe making money.			
4. I am trustworthy—and can make wise financial decisions.			
5. I can make wise financial investments.			
Group B			
1. I can make wise financial decisions.			
2. I give myself permission to enjoy having financial resources.			
3. I give myself permission to enoy making luxury purchases for myself and others.			
4. I give myself permission to enjoy making luxury purchases for myself.			
5. I can be rich and still be spiritually oriented.			
Group C			
1. I can be rich and spiritual at the same time.			
2. People can be rich and be spiritual at the same time.			
3. I am comfortable spending money on myself.			
4. I am comfortable investing in myself.			
5. I am comfortable investing in myself and in my future.			

Lack of Positive Statements (Page 11)	Challenged	Info	Cleared
Group A			
1. Having money is not a sin.			
2. Spending money is not sinful.			
3. Spending money on myself is not sinful.			
4. Investing in myself is not sinful.			
5. Investing in myself and my future is not sinful.			
Group B			
1. I can have money and be a godly person.			
2. I can have money and be a godly person at the same time.			
3. God does not want me to struggle financially.			
4. I do not have to struggle financially.			
5. It does not have to be a struggle to be wealthy.			
Group C			
1. It does not have to be a struggle for me to be rich.			
2. It does not have to be a struggle to experience financial prosperity.			
3. It does not have to be a struggle to experience money liberation—now!			
4. It does not have to be a struggle to manifest money liberation.			
5. I am open and receptive to manifesting money—now!			

Lack of Positive Statements (Page 12)	Challenged	Info	Cleared
Group A			
1. I am ready to manifest money liberation—now!			
2. I am willing to manifest my money liberation—now!			
3. Even if I pray for more financial resources—God still loves me.			
4. Even if I ask God for financial help—God still loves me.			
5. Opportunities and encounters can lead to financially prosperity.			
Group B			
1. Inspired ideas and dreams can lead to financial prosperity.			
2. My intuition is capable of leading me to financially prosperous ideas and opportunities.			
3. I am open and receptive to being divinely guided to encounters and situations that can lead to financial prosperity.			
4. I am being divinely guided in all departments of my life—including my finances.			
5. I am not evil for desiring to improve my financial situation.			
Group C			
1. I am not evil for praying—or asking God—to assist me with my financial situation.			
2. My self-worth is not based on the amount of money in my bank account.			
3. I am not wrong, bad, or evil for wanting more money.			
4. I am not wrong, bad, or evil for asking God for what I want—including more money.			
5. I am not wrong, bad, or evil for being rich.			

Lack of Positive Statements (Page 13)	Challenged	Info	Cleared
Group A			
1. I am not wrong, bad, or evil for praying—or asking God to assist me with my financial situation.			
2. It is okay for me to want more money.			
3. It is okay for me to want to be rich.			
4. It is okay for me to ask God for what I want—including more money.			
5. It is okay for me to pray and ask God to assist me with my financial situation.			
Group B			
1. I am okay for wanting to improve my financial situation.			
2. I am okay—and God is okay—with me asking for what I want, including more money.			
3. I am okay—and God is okay—with me praying for financial prosperity.			
4. I am okay for wanting to be ____________.			
5. I am okay with being ____________.			
Group C			
1. God loves me at all times—now and when I become wealthier.			
2. God loves me at all times—now and when I become rich.			
3. God loves rich people.			
4. God loves rich people—including me.			
5. God loves rich and wealthy people.			

Lack of Positive Statements (Page 14)	Challenged	Info	Cleared
Group A			
1. I am able to quickly and easily handle my bills.			
2. I am able to pay money toward by debts.			
3. I feel confident that I can be debt free.			
4. Paying down my debt is something I can do.			
5. It is possible for me to live debt free.			
Group B			
1. I feel I can get out of debt.			
2. I feel confident in my ability to become debt free.			
3. I can become debt free.			
4. Paying down my bills is something I can achieve.			
5. I can have a more positive relationship with money.			
Group C			
1. Paying off my debt does not have to be a struggle.			
2. I can get ahead financially.			
3. I am capable of improving my relationship with money.			
4. I can visualize my debt going down and my savings going up.			
5. I can eliminate my debt, pay my bills, and save money.			

Negative / Challenged Statements

If during divining of the Negative / Challenged Statements, you test *strong* or *yes* for a statement, check the *Challenged* box. These statements contain energetic / vibrational blocks, imbalances within your subconscious / unconscious—and perhaps even within your conscious awareness—that would be beneficial for you to clear and release to be less encumbered by negativity toward yourself and toward your perceived relationship with God.

If you are prompted to divine for more information and/or if there is an indication that the energetic represented within the statement was inherited, make sure to notate it.

While divining, if you get a *weak* or *no* response to the Negative / Challenged statement, you can leave the *Challenged* box clear or mark the box with a 0. (Leaving the box blank makes it easier to spot the checked boxes.) These statements contain the subconscious / unconscious and conscious thoughts, energy, and vibration that resonate as what you hold as *False* or *Not True.*

After doing the clearing and release work, within the *Cleared* box you can either write the date it was cleared, check the box indicating a clearing, or write a C.

Negative / Challenged Statements (Page 1)	Challenged	Info	Cleared
Group A			
1.			
2.			
3.			
4.			
5.			
Group B			
1.			
2.			
3.			
4.			
5.			
Group C			
1.			
2.			
3.			
4.			
5.			

Negative / Challenged Statements (Page 2)	Challenged	Info	Cleared
Group A			
1.			
2.			
3.			
4.			
5.			
Group B			
1.			
2.			
3.			
4.			
5.			
Group C			
1.			
2.			
3.			
4.			
5.			

Negative / Challenged Statements (Page 3)	Challenged	Info	Cleared
Group A			
1.			
2.			
3.			
4.			
5.			
Group B			
1.			
2.			
3.			
4.			
5.			
Group C			
1.			
2.			
3.			
4.			
5.			

Negative / Challenged Statements (Page 4)	Challenged	Info	Cleared
Group A			
1.			
2.			
3.			
4.			
5.			
Group B			
1.			
2.			
3.			
4.			
5.			
Group C			
1.			
2.			
3.			
4.			
5.			

Negative / Challenged Statements (Page 5)	Challenged	Info	Cleared
Group A			
1.			
2.			
3.			
4.			
5.			
Group B			
1.			
2.			
3.			
4.			
5.			
Group C			
1.			
2.			
3.			
4.			
5.			

Negative / Challenged Statements (Page 6)	Challenged	Info	Cleared
Group A			
1. Money is never there for me.			
2. Having no money is God's way of testing me.			
3. I am being punished—and that is why I don't have any money.			
4. No matter how hard I try, money is elusive to me.			
5. I have bad luck with money.			
Group B			
1. It is my lot in life not to be rich.			
2. Wealthy people are bad.			
3. It is bad to be wealthy.			
4. It is my fate to be poor.			
5. God wants me to suffer—and having no money is part of my suffering.			
Group C			
1. I have to work hard to earn money.			
2. Only the rich and wealthy get richer and wealthier.			
3. No matter how hard I work, I can never get ahead financially.			
4. Because I was not born wealthy, I will never become wealthy.			
5. God is withholding money from me.			

Negative / Challenged Statements (Page 7)	Challenged	Info	Cleared
Group A			
1. If I earn more money, I will be taking money away from another person.			
2. People with money are selfish.			
3. If I become rich, I will become selfish.			
4. Money is evil.			
5. People with money are evil.			
Group B			
1. I can never make ends meet.			
2. Bad people have money.			
3. If I have money, I will become bad.			
4. Money destroys people—and it can destroy me.			
5. Money destroys relationships—and can destroy my relationships.			
Group C			
1. It is safer for me not to have money.			
2. It is not safe to be rich.			
3. I never get what I want—including money.			
4. I never get what I need—including money.			
5. I do not deserve to be rich.			

Negative / Challenged Statements (Page 8)	Challenged	Info	Cleared
Group A			
1. I am just a struggling artist.			
2. I believe that the concept of "starving artists" is a real thing.			
3. I am a starving artist.			
4. Because I am an artist, I will never become rich.			
5. All artists struggle financially.			
Group B			
1. I am not worthy of being wealthy.			
2. It is not humble to be rich—and if I am rich, I will not be humble.			
3. It is my destiny to be poor.			
4. It is not my destiny to be rich.			
5. God doesn't like rich people.			
Group C			
1. If I am rich, God will not love me.			
2. The only way for me to be rich is to win the lottery.			
3. I never win.			
4. I always have to work hard for everything.			
5. I always have to scrimp and save.			

Negative / Challenged Statements (Page 9)	Challenged	Info	Cleared
Group A			
1. I can never get ahead.			
2. I am bad with money.			
3. I can't be trusted with money.			
4. If I become rich, other people will treat me differently.			
5. If I become rich, people won't like me.			
Group B			
1. If I become rich, I will lose my money.			
2. If I become rich, I will not be safe.			
3. If I become rich, I will lose everything—including all of my money.			
4. If I become rich, I will lose friends.			
5. If I become rich, everyone will want money from me.			
Group C			
1. People will resent me if I am rich.			
2. I will change for the worse if I become rich.			
3. Having more money will only increase my problems.			
4. Having money causes problems.			
5. Having money will cause problems for me.			

Negative / Challenged Statements (Page 10)	Challenged	Info	Cleared
Group A			
1. Being rich will cause a wedge between me and others.			
2. Money corrupts people—and having more money will corrupt me.			
3. Being rich is sinful.			
4. It is not godly to be rich.			
5. It is more godly to be poor.			
Group B			
1. I have to struggle to make money.			
2. No matter how hard I try, I cannot hold on to money.			
3. No matter how hard I try, I cannot save money.			
4. No matter what I do, I can't get ahead.			
5. I work hard—yet I can't seem to get ahead.			
Group C			
1. The only way to become rich is by investing in the stock market.			
2. Because I do not understand the stock market, I will never become rich.			
3. Because I do not invest in the stock market, I will never become rich.			
4. Because I do not invest in the stock market and I am not a lottery winner, I will never become rich.			
5. To be rich, you have to be born into a wealthy family.			

Negative / Challenged Statements (Page 11)	Challenged	Info	Cleared
Group A			
1. My family is not wealthy—so I will never become rich.			
2. Rich people are lucky people—and I am unlucky.			
3. Rich people are lucky people—and I am not lucky in life.			
4. Rich people are lucky—and I am unlucky with money.			
5. Because I am not rich, everything is stacked against me.			
Group B			
1. Everybody seems to be getting rich—except me.			
2. The rich get richer—and all I do is struggle.			
3. The money game is a game I can't win.			
4. The money game is a game I am losing.			
5. I cannot figure out the money game.			
Group C			
1. I can't do what I love to do and make money.			
2. I can't do what I want to do and become rich.			
3. I have to sacrifice what I want to do for what I have to do to make money.			
4. What I want to do and what I have to do to make money are two separate and different things.			
5. No matter how hard I try, my money situation stays the same.			

Negative / Challenged Statements (Page 12)	Challenged	Info	Cleared
Group A			
1. No matter how hard I try, I am stuck financially.			
2. Money and I are like oil and vinegar—we separate.			
3. Money will cause separation between myself and others.			
4. I am a loser when it comes to money.			
5. If I had money, I would lose it.			
Group B			
1. If I became rich, I would be too tempted to sin.			
2. If I become rich, my relationship with God would change and not in a good way.			
3. It is wrong for me to want to be rich.			
4. It is wrong and bad for me to invest in myself.			
5. It is wrong for me to spend money on myself.			
Group C			
1. It is wrong and bad for me to desire increasing my finances.			
2. I am not worthy of enjoying lavishness and luxurious things.			
3. It is wrong and bad for me to desire lavish and luxurious things.			
4. It is wrong and bad for me to spend money on lavish and luxurious items for myself.			
5. It is wrong and bad for me to spend money on lavish and luxurious items for myself and others.			

Negative / Challenged Statements (Page 13)	Challenged	Info	Cleared
Group A			
1. It is not spiritual to be rich.			
2. People can't be rich and spiritual.			
3. I can't be rich and spiritual.			
4. I can't be rich and spiritual at the same time.			
5. Having money and being godly are mutually exclusive.			
Group B			
1. It is not right for me to invest in myself.			
2. I can't spend money on myself unless and until everyone else is taken care of.			
3. It is sinful for me to spend money on myself.			
4. It is sinful for me to invest in myself.			
5. It is sinful for me to invest in myself and in my future.			
Group C			
1. Wanting money is not spiritual.			
2. Asking God for money is not spiritual.			
3. God doesn't like people that ask or pray for money.			
4. God won't love me if I ask or pray for more money.			
5. God won't love me if I become rich.			

Negative / Challenged Statements (Page 14)	Challenged	Info	Cleared
Group A			
1. I will always be in debt.			
2. I am never able to make enough money to pay toward my debt.			
3. I feel overwhelmed by debt.			
4. Paying down my debt is something I can't do.			
5. It is impossible for me to live debt free.			
Group B			
1. No matter how hard I try, I can't seem to get out of debt.			
2. No matter how hard I work, I can't get out of debt.			
3. I will never be debt free.			
4. No matter what I do, my debt just seems to be increasing.			
5. Always being in debt is my lot in life.			
Group C			
1. The harder I work, the more in debt I become.			
2. I always have been—and always will be—in debt.			
3. Because of my debt, I will never be rich.			
4. I can never get ahead.			
5. Because of my debt, I will never get ahead.			

Chapter 11

Step 5: Eliminate through Energetic Clearing and Releasing

Over the years, I have studied numerous subconscious / unconscious emotional and energetic clearing and releasing modalities. I have even become certified in various clearing and releasing modalities. Additionally, I have been inspired to create more techniques and protocols.

I am sharing two modalities with you in this chapter. The first is what I call the *Brow, Crown, and Down* method; the second I call the *Acu-Points Rub / Tap* method. Neither is superior to the other; they are just two that worked for me. As a first step, you must discern which modality to use.

NOTE: During any energy clearing and releasing session, you may experience some emotional energy releases (tears, crying, laughing) plus other energetic releases (deep sighing, yawning) during the clearing and release process. If this should happen, it simply means that *e-motion* (energy in motion) is occurring. During my own *"GOD Project"* and *Money Liberation Project*, I experienced dreamlike images, intuitive impressions, felt the energy of certain emotions, experienced sound and colors, and received inner messages. If you do not experience a noticeable emotional release or any of what I described that I experienced, it does not mean that a clearing and release did not occur. You can always verify a clearing through divining.

Divining Which Clearing Modality to Use Protocol

The Process:

- Use divining to discern which clearing and releasing modality would be best for you to use at this time.
  - *Brow, Crown, and Down*? (Y/N?)
  - *Acu-Points Rub / Tap*? (Y/N?)

NOTE: If you test *no* (*weak*) for both, discern which other modality to use (for example, one you may be familiar with and have experience with) by using your intuition and divining.

- Discerning suggestions:
  - Connect within. Ask for clarity and guidance regarding which modality to use at this time.
  - After receiving the indication of which modality to use at this time, ask:
    - *Is it safe and supportive for me to continue at this time?* Divine.
- If *yes*, continue. If you get a *no*—stop!
- Refer to ***What to Do if You Get a No (Weak) to Proceed*** on page 80.

Brow, Crown, and Down Method

Both your fingertips and a magnet emit and carry electromagnetic energy, so your tools consist of:

- Your fingertips
- Optional: magnet (This can be a refrigerator magnet.)

Energy Clearing and Release Protocol for All Sessions

- Follow the ***Beginning Session Protocol for All Divining Sessions.***
- Follow ***Divining Statements Protocol.***

- Follow ***Divining for More Information Protocol***.
- Follow ***Divining Which Clearing Modality to Use Protocol***.
- If the ***Brow, Crown, and Down method*** is indicated, proceed.

Energetic Clearing and Release Procedures for Negative / Challenged Statements[8]

This is the procedure to use if, when divining, you test *strong* (*yes*) regarding a Negative / Challenged statement and are guided to use the *Brow, Crown, and Down* method. (This indicates there is resonance between you and the Negative / Challenged energetic.)

The Process:

- Using your fingertip(s), begin by either lightly rubbing in a circle (for a few seconds—approximately five to six small circles) or tapping (approximately five to six times) on the area of your brow / third eye (area between eyebrows and at the center of the forehead).
- Proceed rubbing or tapping at various spots along the meridian line up to your crown (top of the head) and down (the back of your head to behind your neck). Rub or tap along the path described.
- Modifications:
  - Sweep your fingertips instead of tapping. Sweep several times. (I tend to sweep five or six times.)
  - Sweep the magnet instead of rubbing or tapping. Sweep several times.
  - At the same time, state (verbally or silently) one or more of the following statements:
    - "Release. Release. Release."
    - "Be gone. Be gone. Be gone."
    - "I Am releasing blocks *now*!"

---

[8] If the statement energetic is inherited, refer to ***Clearing and Releasing Inherited Energy Protocol for All Statements*** (***Brow, Crown, and Down Method***) on pp. 222–223.

- "I Am free! I Am free! I Am free!"
- Or create something to that effect.

NOTE: Most of the time, I would lightly rub about three to six circles or tap three to six times per point along the meridian path (or three to six fingertip / magnet swipes along the meridian path); other times it would take more than six. When uncertain, I would divine to discern how many circular rubs / taps / swipes would be best. It may vary from time to time. Follow your intuition.

If you are uncertain about any element, divine within yourself. Ask how many times to rub, tap, or sweep to permanently clear and release the energy. After practicing these techniques, you can learn to know, intuitively, how many times to use to rub, tap, or sweep with your fingertips or magnet along the *Brow, Crown, and Down* meridian.

Clearing and Releasing Inherited Energy Protocol for All Sessions (Brow, Crown, and Down Method)

If there was an indication for you to divine for more information and there was an indication that the energy / vibration was inherited, follow this protocol:

The Process:

- Send a blessing to your ancestor while simultaneously:
  - Doing more *Brow, Crown, and Down* rubs / taps / sweeps—more times than you usually would—and the amount you are intuitively guided to do and/or the amount you discern via divining.
  - Additionally, rub or tap more places along the meridian path.
  - Visualize a cord being untied, a chain breaking, a lock opening between you and your ancestor as it relates to

that specific statement, or whatever else comes forward for you.

- You can also state things like:
  - "Release and go in peace."
  - "I honor and bless you. Be at peace. Now release."
  - Or whatever you feel your intuition is guiding you to state.

Confirm the Clearing and Release

- Ask: *Has this been released?* Divine.
- If you get a *strong* (*yes*) response, confirm the release.

How to Confirm the Release of a Negative / Challenged Statement Energetic

The Process:

- Say the statement (either verbally or silently) and then divine again.
- You should test *weak* (*no*).
- If you test *weak* (*no*) to the Negative / Challenged statement,
  - Ask: *Is it safe and supportive for me to continue at this time?* Divine.
  - If you get a *strong* (*yes*) response, continue.

NOTE: If you still get a *strong* (*yes*) response to the Negative / Challenged statement—stop!

- Ask: *Is it safe and supportive for me to continue at this time?* Divine.
- If you get a *strong* (*yes*) response,
  - Restate your intention to release the Negative / Challenged energetic.
  - Rub, tap, or sweep more times.

- ▲ Remember: If this was an inherited energetic, the clearing and releasing will require more rubs / taps / swipes.
- ▲ Say the statement (either verbally or silently) and then divine again.
  - ◊ You should test *weak* (*no*).

ANOTHER NOTE: If you still test *strong* (*yes*) for the Negative / Challenged statement energetic or get a *weak* (*no*) response after asking if it is safe and supportive to continue at this time, follow the same protocols explained in ***What to Do if You Get a No (Weak) to Proceed*** on page 80.

Energetic Clearing and Release Procedures for Lack of Positive Statements[9]

This is the procedure to use if, when divining, you test *weak (no)* regarding a positive statement using the *Brow, Crown, and Down* method. (This indicates there is dissonance / non-resonance between you and the positive energetic.)

The Process:

- While rubbing or tapping each meridian point, or swiping along the meridian pathway, you can say (either verbally or silently)—following your Intuition / Inner Guidance regarding which statement to say, when to say it, and so on—one or all of the following statements:
  - "It is safe for me to experience ____________________." Example: "It is safe for me to experience being rich."
  - "I welcome the energy of ____________________ now!" Example: "I welcome the energy of *money liberation* for me now!"

[9] If the statement energetic is inherited, refer to ***Clearing and Releasing Inherited Energy Protocol for All Statements (Brow, Crown, and Down Method)*** on pp. 222–223.

  - "It is for my maximum benefit to accept and experience ___________ now!"
    Example: "It is for my maximum benefit to accept and experience financial prosperity for myself now!"
  - And/or whatever else you feel, intuitively, you want to state ...
- Now, specifically address the blocks and/or imbalances:
  - "It is safe for me to remove all blocks and imbalances toward experiencing ___________ now!"
    Example: "It is safe for me to remove the blocks and/or imbalances toward experiencing financial prosperity now!"
  - And/or something similar. Follow your intuition.

Confirm the Clearing and Release Protocol

- Ask: *Has this been released?* Divine.
- If you get a *strong* (*yes*) response, confirm the release.

How to Confirm the Release of a Lack of Positive Statement Energetic

The Process:

- Say the statement (either verbally or silently) and then divine again.
- You should test *strong* (*yes*) for the positive statement energetic.
- If you test *strong* (*yes*) to the statement,
  - Ask: *Is it safe and supportive for me to continue at this time?* Divine.
  - If you get a *strong* (*yes*) response, continue.

NOTE: If you still get a *weak* (*no*) response to the positive statement—stop!

- Ask: *Is it safe and supportive for me to continue at this time?* Divine.
- If you get a *strong* (*yes*) response,
  - Restate your intention to release the Lack of Positive energetic.
  - Remember: If the statement's energetic / vibration is inherited, refer to ***Clearing and Releasing Inherited Energy Protocol for All Statements (Brow, Crown, and Down Method)*** (pages 222–223).
  - Say the statement (either verbally or silently) and then divine again.
  - You should test *strong* (*yes*).

ANOTHER NOTE: If you still test *weak* (*no*) for the positive statement energetic or get a *weak* (*no*) response after asking if it is safe and supportive to continue at this time, refer to ***What to Do if You Get a No (Weak) to Proceed*** on page 80.

Always remember: Be gentle with yourself. Drink lots of water. Try again another day.

Acu-Points Rub / Tap Method

Below are the procedures I follow when I use the *Acu-Points Rub / Tap* method.

Tools:

- Fingertips
- Awareness of some meridian acu-points: (partial listing)
  - Top of the head / crown
  - Third-eye area / top of brow (center forehead above eyebrows)
  - Side of the eye / temple

- o Under the eye
- o Under the nose / above the lip
- o Under the ear
- o Middle of chin
- o Below collar bone / below where the collarbone sticks out
- o Front side of armpits
- o Sides of rib cage
- o Side of palm (below index finger)
- o Web between index finger and thumb
- o Hugging the wrist with opposite hand

NOTE: Again, not all of these points need to be rubbed in a circular motion or tapped. Additionally, other points can be rubbed or tapped. Some systems use more, some use less.

If this technique is new to you, I suggest you first practice rubbing or tapping on all of the points listed. I tend to rub or tap the following: crown, brow area, side of the eye, under the eye, under the nose / above the lip, middle of chin, below collar bone, side of palm, index / thumb web (sometimes), as well as hugging the wrist of one hand with the other hand. Sometimes I rub or tap additional areas; sometimes I rub or tap very few areas.

Energy Clearing and Release Protocol for All Sessions

- Follow the ***Beginning Session Protocol for All Divining Sessions.***
- Follow ***Divining Statements Protocol.***
- Follow ***Divining for More Information Protocol.***
- Follow ***Divining Which Clearing Modality to Use Protocol.***
- If the ***Acu-Points Rub / Tap Method*** is indicated, proceed.

Energetic Clearing and Release Procedures for Negative / Challenged Statements[10]

This is the procedure to use if you, when divining, test *strong* (*yes*) regarding a Negative or Challenged statement—indicating a resonance between you and the Negative / Challenged energetic—and feel guided to use the *Acu-Points Rub / Tap method.*

The Process:

- Using your fingertips, begin lightly rubbing or tapping (five to six circular rubs or taps ... or as many times as you are intuitively directed to rub or tap, or however long it takes for you to complete one of the statements below) on the meridian points suggested or indicated.
- While rubbing or tapping on each point, say (verbally or silently)—following your Intuition / Inner Guidance regarding which statement to say, when to say it, and so on—one or all of the following statements:
    - "Release. Release. Release."
    - "I release this energy from me now."
    - "Time to let this go."
    - "It is for my highest good to release this now."
    - "It is safe for me to let this go now."
    - "I Am ready, willing, and able to let go of this now."
    - Or say whatever else you feel, intuitively, you want to state.

Clearing and Releasing Inherited Energy Protocol (Acu-Rub / Tap Method)

If there was an indication for you to divine for more information and there was an indication that the energy / vibration was inherited, follow this protocol:

[10] If the statement energetic is inherited, refer to ***Clearing and Releasing Inherited Energy Protocol for All Statements*** (***Acu-Points Rub / Tap Method***) on pp. 228–229.

The Process:

- Send a blessing to your ancestor while simultaneously doing more acu-point rubs / taps—more times than you usually would—and the amount you are intuitively guided to do and/or the amount you discern via divining.
- Additionally, rub or tap more acu-points along the meridian path.
- Visualize a cord being untied, a chain breaking, a lock opening between you and your ancestor as it relates to that specific statement, or whatever else comes forward for you.
- You can also state things like:
    - "Release and go in peace."
    - "I honor and bless you. Be at peace. Now release."
    - Or whatever you feel your intuition is guiding you to state.

Confirm the Clearing and Release

- Refer to ***How to Confirm the Release of a Negative / Challenged Statement Energetic*** (pages 223–224).

Energetic Clearing and Release Procedures for

Lack of Positive Statements[11]

This is the procedure to use if, when divining, you test *weak (no)* regarding a positive statement using the *Acu-Points Rub / Tap* method. (This indicates there is resonance between you and the Negative / Challenged energetic.)

The Process:

- While rubbing or tapping on each meridian point, you can say (either verbally or silently and following your Intuition / Inner Guidance concerning which statement to say and when to say it—or something similar) one or all of the following statements:

[11] If the statement energetic is inherited, refer to ***Clearing and Releasing Inherited Energy Protocol for All Statements (Acu-Points Rub /Tap Method)*** on pp. 228–229.

  - "It is safe for me to experience ____________________."
    Example: "It is safe for me to experience *money liberation*."
  - "I welcome the energy of ________________ now!"
    Example: "I welcome the energy of financial prosperity now!"
  - "It is time for me to experience ______________ now!"
    "Example: "It is time for me to experience *money liberation* now!"
  - "It is for my maximum benefit to accept and experience ________________ now!"
    Example: "It is for my maximum benefit to accept and experience financial prosperity now!"
  - "I Am ready, willing, and able to embrace ______________ now."
    Example: "I Am ready, willing, and able to embrace the idea that I am worthy of financial prosperity now."
  - And/or whatever else you feel, intuitively, to state ...

- Also, you can specifically address the blocks and/or imbalances:
  - "It is safe for me to remove all energetic blocks and imbalances toward experiencing ____________ now."
  - "I Am ready, willing, and able to clear and release any and all blocks toward ____________ now."
  - "It is time to let go of all blocks and imbalances preventing me from experiencing ____________ now."
  - And/or something similar. Follow your intuition.

Confirm the Clearing and Release

- Refer to ***How to Confirm the Release of a Lack of Positive Statement Energetic*** (pages 225–226).

Other Energetic Clearing Modalities and Sources of Information

As mentioned several times, there may be another / other clearing and releasing modality / modalities you may be directed to use. You may also be directed to change the healing modality to use for each clearing session. As always, use your Intuition / Inner Guidance and divine to discern which energetic clearing and release modality would be most beneficial at the time and each time you do this work.

Again—and as always—other sources of information are going within, directly asking God / Spirit / Highest Power, and using your intuition. Ask for guidance and support. Affirm clarity.

BOTTOM LINE: Go within. Meditate. Breathe. Be still. Be open. Be flexible. Connect with your Intuition and Inner Guidance—the Divine Within.

Additional Support

Journaling is a useful way to express and explore your thoughts, feelings, experiences, and insights. It is also a wonderful way to document and track your progress.

Journal Your Session Experiences

In your journal, make notes regarding the experience of your session—both during and immediately after each session. Sometimes, while doing this type of work, you receive epiphanies, inspirations, revelations, images, and/or messages. Document these, as they may provide material to further explore in subsequent meditations, and this information can be used to create intentions, affirmations, and so on.

Journal Your Dreams

Additional information may also be revealed during your dream state. Always keep a journal and pen near your pillow or bedside.

Grab them prior to or as soon as you open your eyes, and begin writing whatever you can gather and/or recall. (Opening the eyes for too long before writing can result in losing the message, as another type of processing of sensory information kicks in.)

Do not worry about your handwriting or your spacing on the page. Write key words, impressions, phrases, descriptive images—anything and everything you can possibly recall. These notations can also be explored in more depth in your meditations and used to inform your intentions, affirmations, and prayers.

Chapter 12

Step 6: Empower

At this point in your *Money Liberation Project*, I want to offer suggestions to support you in positively reinforcing and shoring up any and all new and positive perspectives regarding money, financial prosperity, your *money liberation*, God / Spirit / Your Highest Power, money, and so on. Below are all things I have used and have found to be successful for reinforcing lessons learned, insights gleaned, and money relationship "improvements" (on my part).

Revisit and Review

After being vulnerable and putting heart-centered time, energy, and focus on your transformation, I believe it is good to positively reinforce and support such work. One way to do this is by reviewing your tracking notes. Notice any improvements?

Journal about your observations of the review of your tracking.

Journal (cont.)

Journal (cont.)

Journal (cont.)

Another way to support yourself is to review your progress. Retake the Stress / Challenge Evaluation (see page 92).

Journal about any changes you noted between your before and after Stress / Challenge Evaluations.

Journal (cont.)

Journal about how you perceive money and your relationship with money now. *How do you feel? What do you think?*

Journal (cont.)

Journal (cont.)

Additionally, journal what you are grateful for. (You can also make a list starting with the words "I Am grateful for ...".) State gratitude for anything and everything—including what you learned as a result of doing your *Money Liberation Project*—and your gratitude for what you have learned about you, money, God and money, and so on.

Journal (cont.)

Journal (cont.)

Journal (cont.)

Continuing Supportive *Money Liberation Project* Relationship Practices

Maintaining a positive relationship—with anyone or anything—requires time, energy, effort, positive focus, commitment, practice, and honesty—just to name a few key elements. The same is true as it relates to improving your perceived relationship with money.

Here are some ways I have incorporated these elements:

- Meditating—*listening* to God / Spirit / Your Highest Power / Inner Voice / Intuition
    - I set the intention to meditate at least two or three times a week between ten and twenty minutes per session. I schedule that time on my calendar and do it while seated in a chair with good back support and with my phone turned off and no other external distractions.
- Tracking
    - Track delightful synchronicities—what I call "God winks," which are times I experience
        - being in the flow with money;
        - the influx of financial resources;
        - inspired ideas that can be monetized;
        - inspired connections that can lead to financially profitable ventures, collaborations, and so on; and/or
        - excitement and joy at the idea of experiencing *money liberation*—and that it could really happen for me.
- Journaling
    - Writing about what I am tracking and my tracking experience
    - Writing / expressing my thoughts, feelings, ideas, and gratitude

  - Documenting my session experiences, dreams, impressions, messages, and revelations

    NOTE: I am not a very consistent journal writer. I do, however, experience value when I actually journal.

- Checking within—connecting with myself; connecting with Spirit; connecting with Spirit and myself—as a whole
  - I do this several times a day. I have an application on my computer that could be programmed to chime at desired intervals. When I heard the chime (approximately every two hours from 9:00 a.m. to 5:00 p.m.), I would:
    - stop what I was doing;
    - stretch;
    - look at my *Money Liberation Project* collage / vision board;
    - take a few deep breaths;
    - say favorite money mantras / affirmations / declaration and claiming statements silently within and/or out loud;
    - say a prayer; or
    - simply say, "Hi God! It's me, Linda!"
  - Other times, I visualize money
    - flowing to me;
    - falling from the sky;
    - as a *huge* number in my bank account statement;
    - in my mail, receiving checks for *huge* sums of money;
    - coming out of my computer screen, my cell phone, and so on.
  - I stretch again and resume what I am doing.
- Writing positive affirmations / declaring and claiming statements

- I always enjoy this activity. I invite my playful inner child to assist me with creating and reciting what was created—with great vim, vigor, enthusiasm, and joy.

- Setting positive intentions / declaring and claiming statements upon waking, regarding my perceived relationship with money
    - Upon waking and prior to opening my eyes, I ask myself a version of these questions while focusing on the idea of money:
        - *What do I want to* be *today?* (Joyful? Playful? Generous? Productive? Creative? Expansive? Open to possibilities?)
        - *What do I want to* experience *today?* (Joy? Productivity? Inspiration? Creativity? Playfulness? Being "in the flow"? Possibilities? Expansiveness? *Money liberation*? Safety and comfort? Income generation?)
        - *God, what would you like me to experience today?* (Receiving money? Donating money?)
        - *God, what would you like me to learn today?* (Being open to financial prosperity? Changing my money mindset?)
        - *God, as it relates to money, what qualities would you want me to embody today?* (Assuredness? Confidence?)
- Upon waking, expressing gratitude
    - Express gratitude (silently, verbally, and/or via journaling) for anything and everything—including the financial resources I already have.
        - I begin with the statement *"I Am grateful for ..."* and then state whatever comes forward.
- Prior to sleeping, expressing gratitude

- Express gratitude (silently, verbally, and/or via journaling) for anything and everything—including experiencing the benefits of the financial resources already available to me.
- I begin by thinking about my environment or looking around my bedroom seeing what I already have

o A bed

o A roof over my head

o Clothes to wear

- I start with this statement: *"I Am grateful for ..."* and then state whatever comes forward.

• Also prior to sleeping, setting my intentions to use this time to enable my subconscious mind to relax during my sleep time and to enable blocks and/or imbalances to be cleared and released in an easy and gentle manner—and to wake refreshed and invigorated.

o First, I thank God for the day.

o Next, I say a prayer and then set my intentions of effortless clearing, releasing, and healing while my body experiences reparative and restorative sleep.

o I set my intention to awake refreshed, replenished, and renewed.

NOTE: Prior to being a student at USM, I sporadically set intentions before going to sleep. While a student, this became a nightly practice. It has now become a supportive habit.

• Socializing with energetically and spiritually uplifting people—and engaging with people who are forward-facing, success-minded, financially optimistic, and supportive.

o This is such a fun and supportive step. I love having conversations that matter with members of my spiritual "tribe"—"my peeps." I enjoy being silly and playful with them, too.

- Strategize with a financial planner
- Educate yourself about finances and investing by
    - Taking courses;
    - Watching instructional videos;
    - Reading financially related articles and books;
    - Talking with financially successful individuals; and/or
    - Leaning in to new types of investments (i.e., cryptocurrency).
- Keep track of your personal finances
    - Do monthly reviews of statements
        - Set criteria for income amounts to place in
            - Savings
            - Investments
            - Retirement accounts
        - Set criteria for outflow
            - Prioritize bills
            - Donations, tithing
            - Strategize for vacations, holiday spending, and so on
- Create your new money story and include
    - What being wealthy and/or financially prosperous means to you
    - How you are currently experiencing great riches and wealth
- Getting additional support on all levels
    - Spiritual: seeking spiritual counseling, prayer support
    - Some churches offer supportive spiritual counseling, prayer services, and prayer support. I know of a church that has a prayer hotline. I sometimes ask my friends

for "Love and Light" support—and I provide the same for them. I am on several prayer lists. I also fill out a request for prayer support if the church I am visiting offers one.

- If candles are offered, I also light a candle while stating my prayer and/or intention.
- Seeking additional energetic healing. I love learning about healing modalities. I love that I can find a myriad of Spirit-connected and Spirit-gifted facilitators of healing. In addition to being blessed to have studied and become certified in various healing modalities myself, I love experiencing the gifts of clearings, releasing, healing, and upliftment facilitated by others.

- Being of service to others
    - Every time I volunteer, I set a service intention. Offering selfless service in support of others is a wonderful way to practice connecting with God / Spirit / Your Highest Power, being in the flow, giving and sharing what you already have (time, resources), being generous, and so on—in a conscious way.
    - I view serving others as an opportunity to practice being God's hands and feet and God's Mind and Heart.
    - Service is a wonderful way to practice generosity. You can donate your time and/or funds to people, causes, movements, and organizations you care about.
    - By giving, you are able to practice—and experience—expansiveness while serving others.
        - Services expands hearts by
            - creating connections;
            - expanding peoples' visions to heart-centered possibilities;
            - providing an opportunity to give from your heart and soul; and/or

- ▲ creating a sense of having more than enough—even an "abundance" of resources—that you can give to others—*abundantly*.

Regardless of your religion or denomination, here are some additional things you can do to support yourself in connecting to God Within and God Throughout:

- Chant, recite mantras
  - I use what I have learned from various spiritual venues that resonate and invoke a more positive, uplifted, and open state within me.
  - I also enjoy creating my own chants and mantras.
- Sing or listen to spiritually uplifting songs—and money related songs—that make me smile and laugh
  - My go-to playlist is Christmas music—regardless of what season it is! Gospel music also inspires and delights me.
  - I also enjoy writing my own lyrics to songs. I get the karaoke versions of certain songs and enjoy singing the new lyrics I create for them.
- Listen to informative, educational, inspirational, and uplifting recordings (audiobooks, podcasts, TED Talks)
  - I love listening to audio recordings of "rags-to-riches" stories, workshops, and talks.
- Read business and financially oriented books and articles from a variety of sources
- Attend business and finance-based inspirational and uplifting workshops, seminars, and training programs
  - I enjoy attending workshops given by my favorite transformation-oriented and spiritually oriented authors. It gives me an opportunity to incorporate what they have written about on another level—in a more interactive way and with a community of fellow seekers.

    - I took financial prosperity workshops and courses at a local church that resonated with me.
    - I take spiritually oriented, financial prosperity online classes and workshops.
- Attend spiritually inspirational services and celebrations
    - This recharges my spiritual battery and provides me an opportunity to be of service by donating some funds and/or serving others in some capacity.
- Ask questions and seek answers
    - I go within and ask God for answers and insights regarding my questions, confusion, concerns—about anything and everything, including money.

Prior to beginning each and every clearing session and after following the standard protocol that I shared with you, I visualize myself standing before God / Spirit / My Highest Power and asking questions. Now that I have become more comfortable with this process, I actually visualize myself sitting in front of God—and having an actual dialogue.

Remember ...

> Ask and it will be given to you; seek and you will find; knock and the door will be opened to you. For everyone who asks receives; the one who seeks finds; and to the one who knocks, the door will be opened. (Matthew 7:7-8, NIV)

Chapter 13

Moving Forward

Change can be quite threatening to some people. Any change.

After releasing old and ineffective energy blocks and imbalances (both conscious and unconscious / subconscious) and incorporating new insights and ways of being within yourself (toward money, your *money liberation*, others, and to life and living in general), moving forward is the next step.

Moving forward takes courage. That is especially true when unhappy, angry, fearful, financially stuck, frustrated, and judgmental people notice a shift in you—and with your improved financial prosperity. Some may feel threatened because your reaction to the interaction between the two of you is no longer the same or predictable. Your responses and interactions become unpredictable—and this can be quite unsettling for them. Some may want to remind you of your past in an attempt to keep you bound, captive, held hostage, and forever tethered to your past. They want to define you based on their perceptions / misperceptions of their—and your—past. They view you—and life, in general—through their rearview mirror.

Actually, all this does is keep *them* tethered to *their* own past—*their* own misperceptions and distortions based on *their* own inner negativity. They are trying to hoist their negative perceptions of their past into their—and your—present and future. These people want to hold on to their own past and use it as a weapon to keep you in place. That "place" happens to be within their own negativity, judgments, unhappiness, frustration, level of "stuck-ness," and fear. They think they can use that "place" as leverage to control you. In fact, it only serves as a means of constriction and confinement within them. It holds *them* hostage and bound to *their* past.

Others, who have not yet moved forward themselves, may say things—and react—with these words, attitude, and energetic:

- "How dare you rock the boat!"
- "I remember when you said (or did) ____________."
- "You acted like ____________."
- "I remember the time when you were ____________."
- "I will never forget the time when you said (or did) ________."
- "I will never forgive you for ____________."
- "I will never forget or forgive you for the time when you ________," and they may be feeling / thinking:
    - "If you succeed, I will be left behind," and/or
    - "If you are financially successful, you will leave me behind."

Energetic Qualities of Moving Forward

- Having determination / resolve
- Embracing fortitude / perseverance
- Loving and caring for everyone involved, including yourself
- Releasing
- Allowing
- Being nonjudgmental

Examples of Moving Forward

When confronted and challenged by those in fear, resistance, frustration, and judgment who are experiencing anger, unhappiness, feeling "stuck" and/or limited, and are discontent with their own lives, it would behoove you to focus your energy and attention on your continuing transformation. Focus on your intentions, declaring and claiming, and commitment to your growth and upliftment. In other words, "Keep on keeping on."

A more positive way to reframe or perceive others' reactive and negative responses to your evolution can be applied to the ways people react (such as anger, disturbance, reactiveness, defensiveness, and attacking). Neutrally observing the amount and/or intensity of others' negative reactions can be a great tool for you to measure how much you have grown, been uplifted, transformed—and liberated. More simply stated, the strength of others' negative reactions can reflect, proportionally, the degree to which you have transformed.

Some things to consider: Sometimes "allowing" and "releasing" may mean allowing other people to be themselves and releasing any and all judgments you may have against *them* for how they are reacting to your transformation and liberation. At times, it may mean releasing the relationship—allowing your continuing upliftment, transformation, and *money liberation* with freedom from their negative reactions, energy, repercussions, and interference.

BOTTOM LINE: At all times, try your utmost to be loving and caring toward everyone—especially those who are on a different path in life. May *everything* serve as a blessing and lesson for you. Again, at all times, try your utmost to be grateful for the gifts and blessings that negatively reactive people have been in your life, and bless them and their journeys through life. Move forward on your own path—loving them *and* yourself—along the way.

Questions and Responses

Question: How do I refer to exact statement numbers? Is this example correct? Negative / Challenged Statement, Page #3, Group C, Statement #4

Response: Keep things simple and easy. You can create a way of documenting that works for you. This is how I do it: using the same statement above, I document it as: –3C4. If it were a Lack of Positive Statement: +3C4.

Q: Can any of the *challenges* be inherited?

R: Yes. You can inherit a lot from your ancestors—including lines of energy.

It is possible that you can inherit negative lines of energy from your ancestors on either side of your family regarding both the presence of Negative / Challenged energy and the Lack of Positive energy.

(**NOTE:** It is also possible to have inherited positive lines of energy, too!)

Q: How will I know if these *challenges* were inherited or not?

R: You can always ask by going within and divining for the answer. Most likely, if you need to know additional information (for example, maternal or paternal side; male or female relative), it will be indicated with a *strong* or *yes* response at the time you ask whether or not you need to know additional information. If you do get a *strong* or *yes* response, you can discern through divining:

- *"Was this issue inherited?"* (Y/N)

If you continue to get a *yes* response, you can continue to discern through divining:

- *"Maternal side?"* (Y/N) *"Paternal side?"* (Y/N)

After this, continue to ask if you need to know additional information or not.

If you get a *weak* or *no* response, you do not need to know additional information. I suggest you simply move on.

Q: If something is found to be inherited, does that mean a direct bloodline kind of thing?

R: Yes and no.

- Yes: Just as one inherits DNA from one's ancestors / lineage, so can one inherit a line of energy.
- No: While you may not have inherited a challenge via your ancestor's / lineage's direct bloodline, you can still "take on" a group's / family's line of energy. For example, if you join or expand into a "new family" through marrying into another family or becoming part of a blended family—or changing religions—you become immersed in the energetic line of that family's / tribe's / religious group's belief system. That energetic line may be taken on—embraced, so to speak. It can permeate and/or hover within and around your energy field. This means you can inherit (or take on) an energy line of a belief system that you were not born into—without a direct physical, bloodline inheritance.

NOTE: Even within a family / "tribe" / religion, not everyone deals with the same inherited energetic—or energetic statement. Even identical twins may not have the same inherited energetic blocks and imbalances. The reasons for this phenomenon are varied: lessons to be learned, one's individual Soul's path, and so on. Different people and different belief systems refer to this individualization by different terms: one's lot in life, fate, lessons, karma, and so on.

Another way of viewing the concept of an inherited energetic is this: Some people believe that the Soul continually evolves and does so by reincarnating and experiencing many different lifetimes. Again, believing in or not believing in reincarnation is *not* part of this program. I am simply sharing a perspective.

If, however, you do believe in reincarnation, a way of explaining individualization and inheritance of energetic lines of energy is as follows: A *challenged* line of energy can be inherited / carried over from one lifetime to another—until it is finally cleared and released.

Q: If there is a statement with a blank to fill in (for example, +13B4: "I am okay for wanting to be ____________."), what do I do if I have a list with more than one item?

R: Take a moment, go within, and see what comes forward. You might only have one issue come up. If, however, you get a list of things, ask yourself and discern through divining:

- *"Do I have to clear each issue individually?"* (Y/N)

If you get a *yes*, make a list of each issue, write a statement, and energetically clear and release each statement individually. If, however, you get a *no,* you can confirm this by asking:

- *"Can I clear everything all together?"* (Y/N)

You should get a *yes*.

Q: I divined and got the exact same statement to clear twice. What's up with that?

R: You most likely forgot to check (the first time) whether or not you needed to know more information about the energy surrounding the statement. As an example, if the energy was inherited, you need to do more circular rubs or taps, swipes of your fingers or magnet, or more light rubbing on the points along the *Brow, Crown, and Down* meridian pathway again.

Next steps:

- Discern if you need to know any more information.
- If you divine a *yes*, clear again.
- Make sure you do additional circular rubbing, tapping, or sweeps of your fingertips or magnet, or lightly rub the meridian points again, as indicated through divining / your intuition.

If, after following the protocol above, you still get the same statement to clear, it may be that there is a similar energetic that is close to, but not the specific or exact word / emotion / energy / vibration within that exact worded statement, that still needs to be cleared.

After you clear that original statement,

- Go within and ask what the energetic is that needs / wants to be cleared;
- Follow your intuition; and then ...
- After you receive a sense of what that energetic may be, discern through divining:
    - *"Is* (substitute the new word / emotion / energetic in that same statement) *the energetic that needs to be cleared?"* (Y/N)

What comes forward for you, after going within and following your intuition, is most likely what was trying to get your attention by making you go back and revisit a particular statement. On numerous occasions, that is what I experienced.

NOTE: Words are limiting. Sometimes, while some words' energetic vibrations are close or similar, they are not the exact vibration that needs to be released. Another possibility is that some energetic vibrations may have needed to be cleared and released *prior* to the exact energetic vibration being able to come to the fore to be cleared and released. Additionally, this could also be a practical example of the "gatekeepers" at work.

BOTTOM LINE: This is a process. Always be gentle and patient with yourself and your own process as you gently remove various energetic layers to access the core / root of the energetic to clear and release it.

Q: Through divining, I was directed to clear something that I did not test for as something that needed to be addressed. Why?

R: Sometimes, after there has been clearing and releasing of some energy statements' vibrations, other energetic statements—that formerly tested one way—may change. There is a reason for this.

Healing can be described as the unpeeling of a multi-layered onion or the removing of the prickly leaves of an artichoke to ultimately reveal the heart inside. Somewhat similar to the answer to the previous question about clearing the same statement twice, once one layer is cleared and released it may create a space that allows for the other energetic vibration / energy statement to come forward to be cleared and released next. While this may not happen often, it can happen.

SUGGESTION: After you have completed all of your clearings, go to each statement page (Lack of Positive and Negative / Challenged statements). Go within and ask:

- *"Have all the statements that need clearing and releasing on this page been cleared and released?"* (Y/N)
    - If you get a *yes*, all is complete.
    - If you get a *no*, divine which statement(s) need to be cleared and released, and then proceed to clear and release them.
    - Discern, via divining, which needs to be cleared first ... next ... next ...

Q: What did you experience during your clearing and release sessions?

R: There were times when I was excited to do this work. Other times I felt extreme resistance. Sometimes within the same session, I would experience both. Quite often, it seemed like I was on a roller-coaster ride.

Sometimes, just the revealing of the energy statement to work on stirred emotions and energy within. One of my session journal entries reads:

Just upon discovering this was the one [statement] to be worked on, I cried. The energetic of the revealing of this statement was just so intense ... overwhelming ... sad? I did not even have time to mentally process or contemplate the statement's words or meaning. I had a spontaneous outburst of energy—tears. It was somewhat an experience of relief in just the discovery and uncovering of the entrenched [negative] energetic vibration. The emotion did not come from me thinking about the statement— its meaning or implication. My emotion simply arose upon the discovery and revealing of a deeply hidden and embedded energetic block and bringing the block into the Light. Tears of joy, perhaps ...

Q: What did you experience after your sessions?

R: Sometimes I felt sleepy and would take a nap. Other times, I felt lighter—more buoyant energy compared to the denser energy I felt prior to the start of the session. Other times, I felt nothing.

It is important to note that using emotions as a gauge of clearing and releasing is *not* reliable. Always discern, via divining, that a clearing and release has taken place. If you get a *yes*, accept it. Own it. Embrace it. Move on.

Q: What did you do to prepare for your sessions?

R: I did some prep work on all levels.

- Environmentally: I made sure that the space in which I was doing my session was comfortable and quiet and that I would not be disturbed by others. I also made sure that my phone was off.
- Physically: I drank lots of water prior to and after all sessions.
- Mentally: I set intentions.
- Emotionally: I checked my attitude to make sure I was open and receptive to transformation and not disturbed, distracted, preoccupied, or upset by something.
- Spiritually: Sometimes I meditated. Most times, I said a prayer.

Q: What has changed, if anything, as a result of you doing your *Money Liberation Project*?

R: Many things. Within my inner environment, I have experienced greater

- inner peace;
- inspired ideas;
- comfort by releasing the erroneous notion that I can "control" anything;

- sense of being in the flow—not having to plan, alter, maneuver, or manipulate anything;
- relief that I do not have to "process" anything—which only keeps me in my head and stuck within the mental level;
- calmness because there is significantly less inner chatter from my "monkey / munching mind";
- conscious connection to the present—here and now;
- relaxation because I do not have to "figure things out" on any and all levels and in all departments of my life: financial, career, relationships, and so on;
- owning that I am a generous person;
- compassion, for myself and others, and empathy—knowing that we each did the very best we knew how to do given what we knew at each and every stage in our lives;
- playfulness regarding finances;
- openness and receptivity to new ways of becoming financially prosperous;
- opportunities in which to expand my financial resources;
- connections with other financially progressive entrepreneurs;
- envisioning of these connections as potential partnerships / reciprocal win-win supportive relationships;
- acceptance and allowance—releasing the need to harshly judge myself and others—about money and/or anything and everything;
- forgiveness—releasing my past and the past of others—in the context of spending money, "wasting" money, and so on;
- letting go and releasing my perceived "mistakes" / "errors" / "sins" / misperception positions that I have held against myself as it relates to money—especially of being a "have-not" and/or against "haves";

- letting go and releasing the money "mistakes" / "errors" / "sins" / misperceptions of others that I have held against them—how they spend money, "waste" it, and so on;
- excitement about my *money liberation*;
- trust in God / the Universe—that the best and greatest of everything will happen for me and others;
- conscious awareness of my ever-present connection with my Inner Guidance / Intuition / Inner Knowing—aspects of God Within—and with God Throughout;
- conscious awareness that God communicated and continues to communicate with me in a myriad of ways including via Inner Guidance / Intuition / Inner Knowing—about life in general—and specific things—like money;
- deep breathing and the experience of a greater sense of "safety," knowing as a child of the Divine that it is my birthright to inherit "all that is good"—including money;
- acceptance that I am a wise steward of money;
- confidence—knowing that God has my back;
- assuredness—knowing I am a beloved child of God;
- loving—toward God, myself, and others; and
- excitement and gratitude about fulfilling my lifelong dream of becoming a philanthropist.

Those are just a few benefits that come to mind ...

Q: Any other advice or suggestions you can offer?

R: Be gentle with yourself.

- Take a nap if you need one.
- Shower or take a bath after a clearing and release session if that supports you.
- Stop effort-ing, angst-ing, analyzing, figuring things out, processing or overprocessing, perpetuating stories, creating

stories, being harsh with yourself and your path—and the path of others.

- Remember: This is not a monkey mind / figure it out / mental processing task.
- Allow and accept what was and what is—and move on.
- Embrace and own your good and the good of God—and the good you will do with your financial resources.
- Let love and the vibration of loving be your guide in all things.
- When you want to know something, go within—and ask God to reveal God's Truth to you.
- Ask God to reveal God's True Nature to you.
- Remember—If you allow it to be so, you will be guided and supported in this process. God is on your side ... and so am I.

If you are interested in booking private support sessions, visit

www.DrLindaHumphreys.com.

Summary of Divining Steps and Energy Clearing and Releasing Protocols

Below you will find a list of steps and protocols that can assist you with the divining process and with the energetic clearing and releasing during your *Money Liberation Project*.

  - *Brow, Crown, and Down* Method (pp. 222–223)
  - *Acu-Points Rub / Tap* Method (pp. 228–229)
- Confirm the Clearing and Release (p. 223)
- Energetic Clearing and Release Procedures for Lack of Positive Statements Energetic
  - *Brow, Crown, and Down* Method (pp. 224–225)
  - *Acu-Points Rub / Tap* Method (pp. 229–230)
- Confirm the Energetic Clearing and Release (p. 223)
- How to Confirm the Release of a Lack of Positive Statement
  - *Brow, Crown, and Down* Method (p. 225–226)
  - *Acu-Points Rub / Tap* Method (same as the method above)
- Clearing and Releasing Inherited Energy Protocol for All Statements
  - *Brow, Crown, and Down* Method (pp. 222–223)
  - *Acu-Points Rub / Tap* Method (pp. 228–229)
- Confirm the Clearing and Release (p. 223)

NOTE: If after getting repeated *no (weak)* responses to your correct name when attempting to establish your baseline, whether to proceed, or that a clearing took place—stop. Refer to ***What to Do if You Get a No (Weak) to Proceed*** (p. 80).

Some Fun Resources

Discovering Your Sacred Money Archetypes®

I am excited about sharing some fun resources with you. The first is: Discovering Your *Sacred Money Archetypes®*.

Archetypes, as I understand and use this term, are symbolic and iconic representations of personal characteristics and personality traits.

While you may be familiar with the concept of archetypes and are aware of your personal archetypes—did you know that we also have money archetypes? Well—we do!

The *Sacred Money Archetypes®* (SMA) assessment, created by Kendall Summerhawk, is an insightful tool used to assist with discovering your money archetypes. As an SMA Certified Coach, I am delighted to offer the SMA assessment to you—so that you can discover your top money archetype—for free!

Visit:

DrLindaHumphreys.com/Sacred-Money-Archetypes-SMA-Assessment

for more information—and to take your free assessment now!

Business Branding with Archetypes®

If you currently own and/or want to start your own business, another archetype-related resource offering is Business *Branding With Archetypes®*—another insightful assessment tool developed by Kendall Summerhawk.

In addition to having personal archetypes and money archetypes, did you know that your business has its own special and unique archetype super powers? Well—it does!

For more information about how I can assist you in identifying and clearly expressing your business's authentic brand and attracting your ideal clients / customers with your heart and soul-aligned branding and messaging, visit:

DrLindaHumphreys.com/Business-Branding-with-Archetypes

PLUS...

Money Liberation Coaching

Insightful!

Transformational!

Liberating!

Visit:

DrLindaHumphreys.com/Money-Liberation-Coaching

Bibliography

Biblegateway.com, website, https://www.biblegateway.com

Biblehub.com, website, https://biblehub.com

Brennan, Barbara Ann. *Hands of Light: A Guide to Healing Through the Human Energy Field: A New Paradigm for the Human Being in Health, Relationship, and Disease.* New York: Random House, 1988.

Byrne, Rhonda. *The Magic*. New York: Atria Books, 2012. Print.

Chapman University, "Voice of Wilkerson" page (blog), "America's Top Fears 2015," by Sheri Wilkerson, posted October 13, 2015. https://blogs.chapman.edu/wilkinson/2016/10/11/americas-top-fears-2016/

Dictionary.com, "abundance (n.)," accessed July 17, 2021 https://www.dictionary.com/browse/abundance

Dictionary.com, "abundantly (adv.)," accessed July 17, 2021 https://www.dictionary.com/browse/abundantly

Dictionary.com, "prosperous (n)," accessed July 17, 2021 https://www.dictionary.com/browse/abundantly

Emoto, Masaru. *The Hidden Messages in Water*. New York: Atria Books, 2011. Print.

Garman, Che. "Abundance Quotations." Affirm Your Life (blog). http://affirmyourlife.blogspot.com/2011/06/abundance-quotations.html

Goodreads "Abundance Quotes," (website) https://goodreads/quotes/tag/abundance.

Hawkins, David R. *Power vs. Force: The Hidden Determinants of Human Behavior, Author's Official Revised Edition*. San Diego: Hay House, 2012. Kindle edition, Chapter 3.

Hicks, Abraham. "When Launching Creative Rockets of Desire," March 25, 2011, YouTube video, 00:45, https://www.youtube.com/watch?v=kfuszUBXNMc

Hicks, Esther and Jerry. *Ask and It Is Given: Learning to Manifest Your Desires*. San Diego: Hay House, 2006. Print.

Hicks, Esther and Jerry. *The Essential Law of Attraction Collection.* Hay House, 2013. E-book.

Hicks, Esther and Jerry. *The Vortex: Where the Law of Attraction Assembles All Cooperative Relationships*. San Diego: Hay House, 2009. Print.

Humphreys, Linda. *GETTING GOD® ~ "The GOD Project"—6 Steps for Divining Your Way to a More Intimate & Loving Relationship with God.* Inside Out Transformation, 2019.

Humphreys, Linda. *GETTING GOD® ~ The Guidebook—Exploration & Conscious Connection Support for Your "GOD Project."* Inside Out Transformation, 2019.

Humphreys, Linda. *The Energetics of Money Liberation™ ~ 6 Steps for Finding and Releasing Your Blocks to Experiencing Money Liberation NOW!* Inside Out Transformation, 2022.

Humphreys, Linda. *The Energetics of Money Liberation™* ~ The PLAY*book—Support for Your Money Liberation Project.* Inside Out Transformation, 2022.

Lindner, Melanie. "What People Are Still Willing to Pay For." Forbes (website), January 15, 2009, https://www.forbes.com/2009/01/15/self-help-industry-ent-sales-cx_ml_0115self-help.html?sh=3d8776696758

Myers, Lindsay. "The Self-Help Industry Helps Itself to Billions of Dollars." Brainblogger (website), May 23, 2014, https://brainblogger.com/2014/05/23/the-self-help-industry-helps-itself-to-billions-of-dollars/

NPD Group. "Self Help Book Sales Are Rising Fast in the US, The NPD Group Says," (website), January 13, 2020. https://www.npd.com/news/press-releases/2020/self-help-book-sales-are-rising-fast-in-the-us-the-npd-group-says/

Osteen, Joel. *Become a Better You: 7 Keys to Improving Your Life Every Day*. New York: Howard Books, 2009.

Osteen, Joel. *Your Best Life Now: 7 Steps to Living at Your Full Potential.* FaithWorks. 2015.

Summerhawk, Kendall. Branding With Archetypes®. Heart of Success, 2021.

Summerhawk, Kendall. Sacred Money Archetypes®. Heart of Success, 2021.

United Nations University, "Richest 2% Own half the World's Wealth; Study," news release no. 44: December 2006–February 2007, https://archive.unu.edu/update/issue44_22.htm

Williamson, Marianne. *A Return to Love: Reflections on the Principles of a Course of Miracles.* New York: HarperCollins, 1992.

Acknowledgments

Thank you
God / Spirit / My Higher Power—without whom I could not do anything.
I am in awe, deeply humbled, and grateful for
the miraculous positive transformations in my life.

To my teachers and "way-show-ers":
Dr. Seuss (a.k.a.: Theodore Seuss Geisel)
The Pathwork
Dr. Carl Rogers
Dr. Carl Jung
Marianne Williamson
A Course in Miracles
Rev. Dr. Michael Beckwith
Dr. Paul Barrett
Conversations with God
Drs. Ron and Mary Hulnick
Dr. Caroline Myss
Dr. Joe Dispenza
Dr. Robert Holden

To my dear friends, who made me laugh—especially at myself.

To my "spiritual friends"—
my "nudge-rs" / prodders / stackers / "thorns in my side"
through whom I have learned some of my greatest spiritual lessons along the way.
Y'all know who you are. ☺

To Jeff—
a source of an abundance of great love,
joy, fun, adventure, laughter, and support.

And, as always ... Thank you, BABY JESUS!!!
Amen.

About the Author

I am a seeker.

I am a perpetual student.

I make mistakes.

As a seeker and student, I have learned from my mistakes and am now making conscious strides to "choose again," as *A Course in Miracles* suggests.

I believe in releasing any / all perceived internal confines (judgments, misperceptions)—especially related to the past.

I believe in all forms of forgiveness—including self-forgiveness.

I believe in learning lessons, releasing the past—and moving on.

I believe in being grounded in the present moment because this is where the magic happens. I strive to be present—to fully show up and be "all in"—in all I do.

I believe in being more loving and compassionate toward myself and others in the present—which sets the tone for a more love-filled present—and paves the way for a more love-filled future.

I made a commitment to transform—on all levels.

I strive for personal excellence.

I believe in change, transformation, miracles, and the power of Love.

I view my transformed life as a miracle.

I made a commitment to support others in their transformation and support them in experiencing their own miracles.

My zodiac sign is Gemini.

My "birth card" is Ace of Clubs.

My Enneagram test revealed that I have many personality tendencies (with "tied" scores in both my number one and two positions) with lotsa "wings" to support me.

I don't expect other people to "figure me out" because I can't "figure" myself out.

I tell those I love to "strap on your seat belt" and enjoy the ride when they are with me.

I love flowers.
Tulips make me smile.
I love the scent of carnations.
Laughter makes me laugh.
I love to laugh.
I love spending time with friends.
I believe in "retail therapy."
I believe in capital "T" Truth—and justice.
I love new adventures.
I love delightful surprises.
I love traveling and meeting new people.
I love 70 percent dark chocolate, Utz potato chips, and eating Maryland crab ... anything.
I love to eat.

I am an unabashed fan of music from the '80s.
I love my various families, tribes, and peeps.
I love my husband.
I love America.
I love the entire Universe.
I love children.
I love God.
I love "Baby Jesus."
I love you.

Linda Humphreys, PhD
www.DrLindaHumphreys.com

Made in the USA
Monee, IL
08 November 2026

67969860R00162